5 Marks of Biblical Commitment to the Visible Body of Christ

by C. Matthew McMahon

Copyright Information

Table of Contents

Prolegomena:
The Visible Body of Christ

It is saddening to me that the church is in such theological and practical disarray in our day. Theologically speaking, the visible body of Christ across the globe is as intellectually competent to sound Gospel teaching and preaching, as a newborn is to disclose a lecture on Quantum Physics. This is not an understatement. If people cannot articulate important Gospel doctrines, and believe them by faith, how is the church of Jesus Christ going to be built, or grow?

There are a great number of doctrines that comprise systematic theology. The called-out body of Christ, the church, should know them all. They should be able to define and propagate them faithfully to the glory of God. However, since theological obtuseness has set in, this task is easier left undone than disseminated. People would much rather sing a praise song than study theology. It is far easier to follow along in a jingle, than study to show one's self *approved* before God.

One of those systematic doctrines that is more easily left undone is the doctrine surrounding church covenanting otherwise known as *commitment to Christ's visible church*, which surrounds privileges and benefits of church membership under the commands of Christ. Not only is it an extensive task to cover this topic through the *whole* Bible, but is seen today as something that detracts from the *attractiveness* of the church. In this detraction, the church growth movement has quickly cultivated a *memberless church* (a rejection of a real commitment to Christ) and has appealed and marketed this new brand of false teaching to the "individual Christian." Individualism in and of itself is not necessarily an evil thing depending upon the overall context of the discussion. For instance, each person is created by God individually. God creates people *as* individuals. Each individual is one person, not two or three or eight. But individualism can become sinful very quickly. The sin of individualism is always "evolving" to cope with society's current trends and attempts to market the church and the Gospel to a fallen world. One of the ways in which the sin of individualism is continually breaking down the church of Jesus Christ is the manner in which Christians wield it as a sword or license to dictate *how they may or may not live within the bounds of Christ's visible covenant body*, both in the context of their own lives and also within the local assembly of Christ's mystical body. There is a proper use of individualism, but oftentimes it is one of the sins that Christians must take captive and mortify.

One of the forms of individualism which manifests itself as sinful is the current trend in Evangelical churches to "do away" with commitment to the church, covenanting, unity, prayer, support and membership; as if this is simply something the church has "made up" and placed under the guise of "Christian Prudence" to be cast aside when inconvenient. The propagation of a "memberless" church is often at the heart of the "seeker" churches, or church growth movement, where, 100 years ago, there would be no question as to whether membership in the visible local body of Christ was important. Or to take a step back to the Reformation, there was a need to help people understand church covenanting rightly since the Roman Catholic Church had used membership as a license to sin and turned it into a warrant to oppress those ignorant of the Bible in order to keep them under the control of Antichrist (*i.e.* the papal line). In hiding the Gospel from people, they created a superstitious authority structure in which they had absolute power over the life of a communicant. This is the opposite of individualism in the manner we are currently discussing, but worthy of note. Even in the Reformation of the church, the visible outward profession of faith, and the consequent Baptism of a neophyte, or the children of covenanted members, lead to the inclusion of that person in the local body as something which needed to be done, not something which was *automatically* done. This important point is secondary, though, it does reside in the overall scheme of the issue at hand. Whether or not God commands us to covenant with a local church is the heart of the issue, and the Bible affirms this; it does not deny this.

The first step in understanding membership is to make the distinction between the local church visibly manifested, and the "invisible" church of all elected believers both here and in heaven for all time. The true universal invisible church could be defined as follows: "the entire remnant of the redeemed elect from all ages; both on earth and in heaven." The universal church has many characteristics to it, but only one is important for this introduction: it has no geographic location. The universal church currently has no complete, visible manifestation of all elect believers for all time in one place. This will only be the case until the consummation of the ages occurs and the entire remnant of the redeemed shall be with Christ in heaven forever. On the other hand, the *visible manifestation of the invisible church is the local meetinghouse, or local church in a geographical location.* Where the invisible church is wrapped up in a theological proposition, something to be fully realized and consummated in the future, the visible local church is manifested and expressed in individual geographical bodies *now.* Christians are to be committed to them both.

The church is to be unified (of one mind) in the Spirit by way of covenanting. Covenanting is all but lost. In the "good 'ol days" of Scottish Presbyterianism, about 350 years ago, covenanting was at a zenith. Even the *1647 Westminster Confession of Faith* adopted the *Solemn League and Covenant* (1644), which was a document binding the assembly together in order to hold steadfastly the truths they would set down for the good of the church. *It bled doctrinal unity.*

Covenanting (what might be more acceptably called biblical commitment to the church) is something extended out of and from the covenant signs placed on anyone who receives the terms of the covenant in a body of believers. How can the signs and seals of the covenant be administered except by the minister of a covenanted local church? As the *Belgic Confession* states in Article 30 and 31, "We believe that this true Church must be governed by that spiritual polity which our Lord has taught us in His Word; namely, that there must be ministers or pastors to preach the Word of God and to administer the sacraments; also elders and deacons, who, together with the pastors, form the council of the Church; that by these means the true religion may be preserved, and the true doctrine everywhere propagated...therefore every one must take heed not to intrude himself by improper means, but is bound to wait till it shall please God to call him; that he may have testimony of his calling, and be certain and assured that it is of the Lord." *The 1647 Westminster Confession* in Article 27:2 says, "There be only two sacraments ordained by Christ our Lord in the Gospel; that is to say, baptism, and the Supper of the Lord: neither of which may be dispensed by any, but by a minister of the Word lawfully ordained." In the *1647 Westminster Larger Catechism*, question 169 it states, "How hath Christ appointed bread and wine to be given and received in the sacrament of the Lord's supper? Answer: Christ hath appointed the ministers of his word, in the administration of this sacrament of the Lord's Supper, to set apart the bread and wine from common use, by the word of institution, thanksgiving, and prayer; to take and break the bread, and to give both the bread and the wine to the communicants: who are, by the same appointment, to take and eat the bread, and to drink the wine, in thankful remembrance that the body of Christ was broken and given, and his blood shed, for them (1 Cor. 11:23-24; Matt. 26:26-28; Mark 14:22-24; Luke 22:19-20)." If the minister, then, is the one appropriated to dispense the sacraments, that, in and of itself alone, is enough to demonstrate that the visible local body of believers is a covenanted group of specific members in doctrinal unity. Psalm 133:1 says, "Behold, how good and how pleasant it is for brethren to dwell together in unity!" There is no doubt that the organized brethren who dwell together in unity are blessed. Amos 3:3 further says, "Can two walk together, except they be agreed?" Rhetorically answered, "of course they cannot!" And that verse was in particular, dealing with God and the wayward Israelites who rejected his prescribed truth. Acts 4:32 also demonstrates this unity in the New Testament, "And the multitude of them that believed were of one heart and of one soul." In Colossians 2:2 there is a further statement about the manner in which they are knit together, "That their hearts might be comforted, being knit together in love." This unity is not at the expense of doctrine, practical love, and organization. Paul even exhorts us in Ephesians 4:3 that we should be, "Endeavoring to keep the unity of the Spirit in the bond of peace."

Might I interject this: if there were no identifiable visible body then we would never know who is doctrinally like-minded and who is not. Doctrinal like-mindedness is impossible without a visibly organized church and some form of membership to oversee that gathering. We would never know who are *like-minded brethren* and who are dissenters if this were not the case (this was part of the point of Westminster's *Solemn League and Covenant*). We would have no way to know who the covenanted members of the church are unless we simply *guessed*. And how would guessing be helpful? Consistent like-mindedness would be impossible, practically speaking.

Another often-misunderstood aspect of church covenanting or membership is that entrance into the local church is by consent of the church (*i.e.* the elders of the church). Acts 9:26 says, "And when Saul was come to Jerusalem, he assayed to join himself to the disciples: but they were all afraid of him, and believed not that he was a disciple." We will cover this more extensively later on in the chapter on *membership*, but the idea here extends to all aspects of being committed to the church. Unity, public prayer, support of the church, worship in the church, and covenanting in the church would be a nightmare if that were not ordered by God and left solely up to individual discretion. The disciples needed to see fruit before they would accept Saul, later to be Paul the

Apostle, though Saul *wanted* to be part of them and *wanted* to identify with them. Men do not give themselves to the church. God makes them a part of the local body by providence and spiritual giftedness, and men offer themselves to the church. When men give themselves to the church, the church officers "bind and loose" their "keys" of "binding and loosing men" in and out of the fellowship (Christ's point in the passage on binding and loosing, or, *discipline*). The sin of individualism causes men to include or exclude themselves *as they see it necessary.* They become, as the Latin "vagor" states, vagabonds, or wanderers in the assembly as *they* deem fit and as *they* see fit. Authority is, then, not placed on the officers of the church and the covenant of the body, but rather on the individual who deems when they should stay and when they should move on. This awards sin a license, and immorality a greater reign; for when men sin, tempt excommunication, and are caught, they simply move on to the next body of believers to include themselves there; and so on, and so on, and so on.

The Scriptures make a distinction of those who belong to different churches, and who are associated in each location. They were publicly known to be visibly connected with a particular local body. Rom. 16:1 says, "I commend unto you Phebe our sister, which is a servant of the church which is at Cenchrea." Phil. 4:3 says, "And I intreat thee also, true yokefellow, help those women which laboured with me in the gospel, with Clement also, and with other my fellow-labourers, whose names are in the book of life." Col. 4:9 states, "With Onesimus, a faithful and beloved brother, who is one of you." In these instances Pheobe, Clement and Onesimus are singled out as those who are particularly involved and associated with the church at Rome, in Phillipi and Colossae. In Colossians 4:9, Paul is emphatic, "With Onesimus, a faithful and beloved brother, who is one of you." Onesimus is not singled out as one of the elect of all ages, but one of those brethren *at* Colossae. The word Paul uses here is "ek" which is a primary preposition denoting origin (the point where action or motion proceeds). Onesimus' origin, the place where he is out of or where he proceeds from is the unique relationship he has with the church at Colossae. If someone were to point you out, what church would you be associated with *as a covenanted member?*

The local meeting house (or local church) is the visible expression of a defined group of believers and their children in a given geographic location.[1] The geographic location defined the group of believers at that location, i.e. the church which is *at* Laodicea, *at* Ephesus, *etc.* The letter sent by John to the seven churches was not written to believers in heaven. It was circulated among a specific geographic location *in Asia Minor.* This letter was not written to a structure or building, but a group of believers which made up the seven churches in those geographic areas.

---

[1] *cf.* Rev. 2:1, 8, 12, 18; 3:1, 7, 14.

The Scriptures identify a visible religious organism and organization within a given geographic location. This would not be possible if the sin of individuality was given permission. How could the church appoint anyone to a given office within a local church in a geographic position if they did not know the person, or, could not visibly identify their commitment to the body of believers? How could a minister be appointed over a specific group of people, and oversee a specific flock, if the sin of individuality was given license? It would be impossible. The hierarchy of the church becomes immediately irrelevant and chaos would take precedence if individuality were the norm. Preachers and deacons could then be self-appointed. However, the structure of the church necessitates the organization of the church. Without a God-instituted formal structure, any man, or woman for that matter, could appoint himself or herself (as so many do today). If they could appoint themselves, what rights do the congregation have? How could they have *any* visible rights at all (such as choosing or electing officers in the church)? It would be impossible to exclude anyone (even unbelievers) from coming into the church and giving their opinion since there would be no definable fellowship.

It is also very important to note that privileges of the local church are for the local body not the invisible universal church. For instance, gathering together to hear preaching is a privilege of covenanted members;

Acts 2:42 states, "And they continued steadfastly in the apostles' doctrine and fellowship, and in breaking of bread, and in prayers." Who did this? The church at Jerusalem did this. The privileges of the local church are not for the vagabond who wanders in off the street. Communion, pastoral oversight, fellowship among the brethren, and the like, are privileges of those who are members of a visible community of believers and their children, not for those who appoint themselves to membership or those who want to simply include themselves in the visible body of the church. They are for *covenanters* – those who make a public profession based on faith and like-mindedness in doctrinal matters concerning unity.

Mark 1: Gospel Unity

"To whom coming, as unto a living stone, disallowed indeed of men, but chosen of God, and precious, ye also, as lively stones, are built up a spiritual house, an holy priesthood, to offer up spiritual sacrifices, acceptable to God by Jesus Christ," (1 Peter 2:4-5).

In Peter's general epistle, he writes to the churches at large with a message of hope, and with a message of practicality. He had told his readers to listen to practical reasons for the pursuit of holiness. The elect had been saved through the grace of the Father, the knowledge of Christ, sanctified by the Spirit, and this is all done, "unto obedience." Such obedience is covered in Christ's holy blood, where they are sprinkled, by the blood of the new covenant. In this, God is seen by Peter, and should be by the reader, as blessed forever. Such believers receive an inheritance that can never be shaken or fade, kept by God's power, grounded in true faith.

In all this there is rejoicing for God's priceless provision of salvation. This salvation was foreordained before the foundation of the world in the Covenant of Redemption to save his people from their sins. Christ died, was raised from the dead, and is believed on by faithful, holy Christians, as Peter says, *like you*. These are those who obey the truth by the power of the Spirit. Such truth was preached to them, and they believed it to the saving of their souls.

The pursuit of holiness by casting off sin, and eagerly desiring the pure milk of the Word, which is the catalyst for real growth, is accomplished by reliance on the Spirit illuminating the mind to the truth of the word. More of the word, is more of Christ. More of Christ, gains a more sanctifying effect. Yet this is not solely individual, but it lends itself to corporate growth as a church as each member grows. If one member grows, another grows, and they grow together. Christianity is never for the Lone Ranger.

The text says, "coming to Him as to a living stone." *Coming* means *drawing near* to him. God seeks *worshippers*, a unified congregation of all people together to bring him praise and honor.[1] They come to him *to worship him.* They come to receive from him *life giving power.* Christ is no ordinary temple stone. And even Old Testament temple stones were no ordinary stones. They were specifically designed for the temple, fitted perfectly in their place, so that no hammer or chisel would be heard at the temple site.[2] They were merely fitted together for the spiritual purpose of building the house where God's name would be set.

Christ is the *Living Stone*, a *life-giving* stone. He is the *life-giving* foundation. He gives or imparts life

---

[1] "But the hour cometh, and now is, when the true worshippers shall worship the Father in spirit and in truth: for the Father seeketh such to worship him," (John 4:23).

[2] "And the house, when it was in building, was built of stone made ready before it was brought thither: so that there was neither hammer nor axe nor any tool of iron heard in the house, while it was in building," (1 Kings 6:7).

itself; and those other stones which rest on him gain that life through spiritual transference. They rest on him, trust him, believe on him as *life-giving*. It is somewhat odd to consider that people come to him, draw near to him, for *life* as to a *stone* of life. In contrast to the temple built by hands, Christ is the foundation, the *stone* which is *alive* that holds the building together. He is not lifeless. Even as a regular stone is lifeless, Christ, as a foundational stone is not lifeless. He is the builder of a temple not made with hands, who's builder and maker is God.[3] It is not a mere stone, or a mere building made of material stones. It has spiritual characteristics.

The temple in the Old Testament is made out of materials that such a grand temple should be built from; stone, wood, gold, and such things. But Christ is a *living stone*. One does not ascribe life to things that have no life in them. Stones are inanimate objects. Yet, Christ is *the living stone*. Worship was never about going to a stone temple, but being built into the bride of Christ, being built up into the bride together as living stones.[4] The temple was merely a shadow of such things.

---

[3] "But Christ being come an high priest of good things to come, by a greater and more perfect tabernacle, not made with hands, that is to say, not of this building," (Heb. 9:11). And, compare, "For we know that if our earthly house of this tabernacle were dissolved, we have a building of God, an house not made with hands, eternal in the heavens," (2 Cor. 5:1).

[4] "And I John saw the holy city, new Jerusalem, coming down from God out of heaven, prepared as a bride adorned for her husband," (Rev. 21:2).

Christ is not merely a *place* to worship, he is the facilitator for worship, the vital spark of life and the channel of acceptable existence before God. He is the spiritual foundation to a spiritual building in which he holds all things together. One cannot read Peter's statement here and merely think about a rock or stone. Christ is represented here of the prophetic nature of the capstone which crushes those in rebellion against him, or builds up and holds the building together. "Jesus said to them, "Have you never read in the Scriptures: 'The stone which the builders rejected Has become the chief cornerstone. This was the LORD'S doing, and it is marvelous in our eyes'?" (Matt. 21:42). This is referring to Psalm 118:22-23. "The stone which the builders rejected Has become the chief cornerstone. This was the LORD'S doing; It is marvelous in our eyes." He is not like the temple, not like a stone one finds in a field, or quarry no matter how big or finely chiseled out that stone might be. It is not about size, but about life and vitality. Christ as a stone in this way is *full of life*, a life-giving channel which all other stones that rest on him gain spiritual power. He gives life and strength to all other stones that lay on his foundation in which he holds spiritually together. Like a cell phone that rests on one of those new-fangled charging pads where one simply rests the phone on it instead of plugging it in, that phone receives vitality from the foundation of that pad as it rests on it. Those stones that rest on Christ, that sit on his foundation, receive vitality through the Spirit that Christ sends to them.

This *stone* was "rejected indeed by men." Peter, in referencing Matthew 21 and Psalm 118, conveys the idea here that Christ was rejected and repudiated by men, such as the Pharisees and Sadducees, such as the Romans, and the soldiers that crucified him. Jewish leaders would rather have their stone temple, than the life-giving Anointed Savior. They would rather have *their* kingdom than *God's* kingdom. In his speech with John before the council of the Sanhedrin and High Priest, Peter said, "He is the stone which was rejected by you, the builders, but which became the very corner stone," (Acts 4:11). Such sentiments echo, "He is despised and rejected by men, A Man of sorrows and acquainted with grief. And we hid, as it were, our faces from Him; He was despised, and we did not esteem Him," (Isa. 53:3). The Christ must be rejected in a depraved man's world. One tends to think that in reality, God's Anointed Savior *ought never to be rejected.* This is true enough. But in *a fallen world* what kind of tolerance is expected from carnal minds at enmity with God playing religion in his church? What will happen to God's Savior, his One and Only Son, if the Father sends him to such wicked people? Such an Anointed Savior will always be rejected and repudiated by the rebels who live in enmity against God. Such people hate his ways, his message and his prescriptions for life and godliness. But, their opinion does not practically matter to God in light of his church. Only God's opinion matters; and his Christ is, "chosen by God and precious," Men repudiated him, but God chose him.

Christ is chosen, *picked out*, set down in the decree of God's salvation plan, to work the work of God in time in the power of the Spirit in the Covenant of Grace for his people. He is chosen by the Father and appointed for the everlasting covenant work, pleasing in his sight. "This is my beloved Son, with whom I am well pleased," (Matt. 3:17). "Therefore thus says the Lord God, "Behold, I am laying in Zion a stone, a tested stone, A costly cornerstone for the foundation, firmly placed. He who believes in it will not be disturbed," (Isa. 28:16). God is saying, *I am laying in my church this foundation, this chosen One, my only Begotten Son, the Son of Man who comes from heaven to do my will and establish my covenant among my people.* God lays the foundation down, in this way, and it is established forever. The words, *chosen and precious,*[5] are better translated as one who is *chosen and honored.* God *prized and esteemed* him for his work, and honored him. The relationship between the Father and Son, that is, Christ calling God Father and God calling Christ servant, points to a Covenant of Redemption. Isaiah 49:5–6, "And now the LORD says...'You should be My Servant To raise up the tribes of Jacob, and to restore the preserved ones of Israel; I will also give You as a light to the Gentiles, that You should be My salvation to the ends of the earth.'" In

---

[5] παρὰ δὲ Θεῷ ἐκλεκτόν, ἔντιμον, (1 Peter 2:4).

this servant capacity of the Christ, the whole nature of the covenant exists. Christ calls God his Father, and the Father calls Christ his Servant, empowered without limitation by the Spirit for the work of the everlasting covenant.[6] All of redemption is finalized and made perfect by this Living Stone.

The particulars of the covenant revolve around the contracting parties: Father, Son and Holy Spirit. There are a number of Scriptures that speak to the Father and Son conversing together, or complementing the work of one another in this agreement. The Messianic Psalm, 16:2, says, "O my soul, you have said to the LORD, "You are my Lord, My goodness is nothing apart from You, (*cf.* verse 10)" Such an office, though, is not in the manner in which men may expect. God's plan centers around the reversal nature of the manner in which he works out redemption. Christ does not come as a King, *per se*, but as a suffering Servant (though He is the Prophet, Priest and King in a theological manner); as a spiritual stone, as a living stone for a spiritual house. Carnal people always think the materialistic world is far better. God says that Christ as King over his church is far better. This Stone saves his people, enlivens them, and crushes all his enemies. Isaiah 53:2, "For He shall grow up before Him as a tender plant, And as a root out

---

[6] "Even he shall build the temple of the LORD; and he shall bear the glory, and shall sit and rule upon his throne; and he shall be a priest upon his throne: and the counsel of peace shall be between them both," (Zech. 6:13). "...through the blood of the everlasting covenant," (Heb. 13:20).

of dry ground. He has no form or comeliness; And when we see Him, there is no beauty that we should desire Him." He, that is Christ, shall grow up before Him, that is *God*, in a particular manner to accomplish the desired end of fulfilling the contractual agreement or pact of the Covenant of Redemption. The proposal by the Father (John 10:18), includes a promise and right to ask for completion of the promise upon obedience. If Christ is obedient to the Father, then the Father will provide the necessary means by which the agreement may take effect. This is done by the work of the Holy Spirit in the life of the incarnated Christ. John 10:18 says, "No one takes it from Me, but I lay it down of Myself. I have power to lay it down, and I have power to take it again. This command I have received from My Father." God commands Christ, in a formal agreement, to lay down his life of his own accord. John 12:49, "the Father which sent me, he gave me a commandment." It is done by command, or by the Law, that the Covenant of Redemption is enacted and fulfilled. Psalm 2:8, "Ask of Me, and I will give You the nations for Your inheritance, And the ends of the earth for Your possession." As a result of this obedience, the Father places himself at the disposal of the Son in order to fulfill his mission.

One of the most classic biblical texts of this work of redemption is found in Isaiah 53:10–12, "Yet it pleased the LORD to bruise Him; He has put Him to grief. When You make His soul an offering for sin, He shall see His seed, He shall prolong His days, And the pleasure of the

LORD shall prosper in His hand. He shall see the labor of His soul, and be satisfied. By His knowledge My righteous Servant shall justify many, For He shall bear their iniquities. Therefore I will divide Him a portion with the great, And He shall divide the spoil with the strong, because He poured out His soul unto death, And He was numbered with the transgressors, And He bore the sin of many, And made intercession for the transgressors."

Such a mission is fulfilled by the power of the Holy Spirit though first enacted by the acceptance of the covenant by the Son. John 14:31 says, "But that the world may know that I love the Father, and as the Father gave Me commandment, so I do." And, "For He whom God has sent speaks the words of God, for God does not give the Spirit by measure. The Father loves the Son, and has given all things into His hand," (John 3:34-35). Christ always does what the Father asks, and always accomplishes what he does with a joy to serve. Psalm 40:7–8 states, "Then I said, "Behold, I come; In the scroll of the book it is written of me. I delight to do Your will, O my God, And Your law is within my heart." There is nothing greater to Christ than to serve and fulfill his mission before God to bring him glory. He must perform his work completely and perfectly before God in the Covenant of Redemption to establish it, so that the Covenant of Grace in time will be poured out on his church, and in the power of the Holy Spirit.

Without that work, without that merit and favor gained on behalf of the elect by Christ, no one could ever be saved. This performance by the Son is seen in John 19:30, "He said, "It is finished!" And bowing his head, he gave up his spirit." He finished the work that God gave him to do, and it was satisfactory before the justice seat of God for the elect. God raised the crucified Messiah from death, and placed him on the seat of power. Peter is directing the Christian to come to this Christ, the living stone, rejected indeed by men, but chosen by God and precious.

Peter then says, "you also, as living stones." In some translations they render it "lively" which is somewhat inadequate and antiquated as to its expression. Rather, the Living Stone makes other living stones. They are alive by virtue of Christ's virtue – his life-giving Spirit. The substance of Christian preaching is that the sinners who come to this precious Christ have been made alive and set themselves on the living Stone. Such Christians make up the household of God. Christ is the living stone (1 Peter 2:4 as λίθος ζῶν) who is on the one side the cornerstone underlying the whole building[7] and yet on the other side the stone of stumbling and rock of offence.[8]

Now, Christians are fitted into the building as living stones (λίθοι ζῶντες).[9] Peter strings along a series

---

[7] Isa. 28:16; Psa. 118:22; Mark 12:10.
[8] Isa. 8:14; Rom. 9:33.
[9] 1 Pet. 2:4; Eph. 2:22.

of concepts here: a heavenly temple, holy priesthood, acceptable sacrifices; but these are not materially important. They are *spiritually* important. The church is the house of God, the pillar, the upholder of truth, because the Spirit dwells within it, revelation is committed to it, and good news is proclaimed by it.[10] And it is made up of *a Living Stone* which has set on it other *living stones* which receive their vitality from the Messiah. What are they *becoming?* They "are being built up a spiritual house." It is a *living house* made up of *living stones.* Christ, the foundation, is a Living Stone, and they that are built on him are living stones. They grow together into a spiritual house. This in turn evolves into Gospel growth, and Gospel unity.

Gospel Growth is a *sign of life*, growing from an inward principle by the motion and power of the Spirit. The growth of this house is spiritual. Stones grow, they are built up. This is an amazing illustration. Do stones actually grow? Not in geology, so to speak. But stones in the spiritual temple have a special kind of life, and they grow. That is the kind of life it has – *spiritual life* growing into a full and mature body. And the fulness of its life is in the foundation in which all the other stones come into contact with being built up. Jesus has, "life in himself," (John 5:26). He says, "Because I live, you will live also," (John 14:19). From Christ, the saints in his

---

[10] "But if I tarry long, that thou mayest know how thou oughtest to behave thyself in the house of God, which is the church of the living God, the pillar and ground of the truth," (1 Tim. 3:15).

church are built up in life. All that matters spiritually in the saint, derives from Him. The Apostle Paul said, "I am crucified with Christ, nevertheless I live, yet not I, but Christ lives in me," (Gal. 2:20). Such a house is holy, and in turn designates the service in that house rendered by *priests* – to continue the illustration. Peter says, "a holy priesthood." Those of this house are a holy priesthood, as much as they are living stones. They are designated as a temple, as a house, built as stones which are alive, to having a kind of service, now, in that temple, in that house. In fact, they are built into a holy priesthood. "And you shall be to Me a kingdom of priests and a holy nation," (Exod. 19:6). This is echoed in Revelation where the church is called a kingdom of priests, "and has made us kings and priests to His God and Father, to Him be glory and dominion forever and ever," (Rev. 1:6).[11]

What are these living stones, these priests, to do? Peter says they, "offer up spiritual sacrifices." All that surrounds the corporate body, in unity with one another as a serviceable entity before God, is set down in the phrase "spiritual sacrifices." Hearing, praise, prayer, service of all kinds, obedience, witness, testimony, faithfulness; all the Christian adjectives of service are contained in this as *living to God through Christ.* They are not involved in carnal sacrifices; not earthly, but spiritual. Does God accept them? Peter says, "acceptable to God through Jesus Christ." All that they offer, is made acceptable to God only through the passive and active

---

[11] Compare Revelation 5:10 and 20:6.

obedience of Jesus in his life, death and resurrection as *the* Living Stone. Bring any sacrifice to God and if it is brought in Christ's merit and work, in his power, in his Spirit, with a regenerate heart, God receives it gladly as if Christ himself delivered it to the Father.

Consider, then, that the unity of the saints as his mystical body[12] is founded on Christ as the Living Stone. They are *unified* as One in Christ and are his mystical body together.[13] Christ as the Living Stone, being the author of building in this way, gathers his elect people into one body. As the foundation, he holds up the entire building. In doing this, he builds the building into a full mystical temple, which is his mystical body made of individual members. It is called *mystical* because it refers to all the elect from all of time, whether past, present or those saved in the future.[14] They are all part of this one body. This body includes those in heaven, those going to heaven, and those in the future who will go to heaven. All of them together, make up this mystical body through the Spirit which he sends forth from the Father and the Son. He is the great Shepherd, gathering all his sheep into one-fold. He does this as the High Priest of the Temple, that "Jesus should die for that nation," (John

---

[12] "There is therefore now no condemnation to them which are in Christ Jesus, who walk not after the flesh, but after the Spirit," (Rom. 8:1).

[13] "And hath put all things under his feet, and gave him to be the head over all things to the church, which is his body, the fulness of him that filleth all in all," (Eph. 1:22-23).

[14] See John Brinsley's excellent work, *The Saint's Joint Membership as One Body in Jesus Christ*, published by Puritan Publications.

11:51). And not only for them, but that also he should gather together in one building the children of God that were scattered abroad, scattered even throughout history. Christ has done this *in part* through history, but will further do this until the end of the world. He gathers together his people making them one body, one mystical body, one temple. Ephesians 1:10, "that in the dispensation of the fullness of times, he might gather together in one all things in Christ." All his people are under one head, or as Peter says, into one building, one holy priesthood. Christ is the Head of his Church unifying the people together with one heart. One temple. One priesthood. One nation. One body. "A head over all things to it," (Ephesians 1:22).

Christ participates spiritually with the members of his body through the Spirit which connects and joins them all in one purpose and one spiritual service – to render service that is acceptable to God. As a head guides the nature of the body, so Christ does this with his mystical body, the church. He is there, by his Spirit, in intercession for the temple, set over it, rules it and guides it by his Spirit in spiritual power. He provides for them through his Spirit and gives them all their spiritual influence to work all things before the Father. He motions the Spirit who in turn motions the body to move and work for the kingdom.

In Christ, the members of this mystical body are all united to the head by union and communion through the Spirit. All true living members have this unity.

Christ, being the spiritual head of his mystical body, gives them the Spirit which in turn gives the members the ability to offer spiritual sacrifices through Christ in the fruit of the Spirit. His mystical body is constructed in this way in order that his church may be of the same mind and the same judgment on all spiritual matters. "Now I beseech you brethren, by the name of our Lord Jesus, that ye all speak the same thing, and that there be no divisions among you; but that ye be perfectly joined together in the same mind, and in the same judgment," (1 Corinthians 1:10). The Church, then, ought to be of the same mind, in unity, like-minded, thinking and speaking the same things. Is this not what nature teaches? A human body is of the same mind, and the same thing. It all works together for one purpose driven by the head. Wherever the head goes, the body goes. Any natural purpose is accomplished by the whole man.

Christ's mystical body is often used in the example of a natural body in many ways. This shows that Christ's church should all speak the same thing, all looking the same way, all walking the same way, all with the same interests and service. That is their goal, though the nature of sanctification is a bit different. People spiritually grow at different speeds, but they all grow into the body. They are a unified building. Here Christ's mystical body is built in a new and living way as a temple – where in the physical temple of the Old Testament, they could not do this since the temple, back then, was a shadow of the new temple to come. The priests offered physical sacrifices on behalf of the people as a *type* of the sacrifice of Christ to come. By faith, those Old Testament saints believed in the coming of the Messiah who would fulfill all things through a spiritual dimension for his mystical body. Jesus' death is that which saves, gives vigor and life to the new temple, the new priesthood, all those new living stones; but it was as much the substance of the Covenant of Grace in the Old Testament as it is in the New Testament.

Only in Christ do these spiritual stones, as spiritual priests, go with acceptable sacrifices into a spiritual act of worship. All God's people, in this way, are made priests to God. Every offering given, every song, every praise, every prayer and such, presupposes a priest for offering it. Rev. 1:6, Christ Jesus "has made us kings and priests." Christ is great Prophet, Priest and King who makes his people priests and kings. Yet, in sharing in that holy priesthood, so in a certain sense, being part of his mystical body, Christians are also priests offering sacrifices through him. This is in a *spiritual sense.* Their acceptability is made through their anointing, their power and motioning from the Holy Spirit, and Christ, then, communicates with them in his offices in a unified manner. Peter describes the church as both in 1 Peter 2:5, "a holy priesthood to offer sacrifices to God," and in 1 Peter 2:9 he calls them "a royal priesthood." They, in fact, minister before the Lord in *acceptable sacrifices.* They are the building being founded on Christ, and they are the priests offering holy sacrifices in acceptable service.

Through unity in the Spirit they are made acceptable in all they do as a result of the application of Christ's work to, in and through them. It is all the fruit of the Spirit.[15] It is opposite to their depraved fruit.[16] It is *his* fruit, worked through them, in an anointing of power and covered in the blood of Christ.

The church is a single building, brought together in unity through Christ, founded on his work, and motioned to service that is acceptable by his Spirit, or at least, it should be. Take notice, then, of one further point under this head. The people *are* the temple. Often Christians today adorn the church sanctuary with the shadow of temple ceremonies; pictures, decorations and such that give them a sense of "religiosity". This ought never to be the case. To God, *the people* are the adornment. They are the living stones. The physical temple and its ceremonial shadows have no place, in any way, in these end times. There is no need for a physical temple at any further time. Now, it is a new and living way in Christ as a temple of believers in one body that makes up the spiritual building.

Also, the local meeting house or church building is not modeled after the physical temple. The church (those called out of the world together into Christ's body) is modeled after the *synagogue* in which believers are made *into* a living temple, a living mass of stones on the living foundation of the spiritual temple in these

---

[15] Gal. 5:22-23.
[16] Gal. 5:19-21.

New Testament times. They are now, a holy nation and a holy priesthood unified together. They are a unified priesthood.

When discussing the Priesthood, one cannot but consider the idea of being separated, or *holy*, for God. When something is "holy" it is separated from a normal use for something that is special. "And you shall be holy to Me, for I the LORD am holy, and have separated you from the peoples, that you should be Mine," (Lev. 20:26). "Therefore "Come out from among them And be separate, says the Lord. Do not touch what is unclean, And I will receive you,"" (2 Cor. 6:17). In terms of something that is holy in relationship to God, it means that it is utterly separated *to God's service* and *for his glory,* which means it cannot be tainted with sin or imperfection. "Now therefore, if you will indeed obey My voice and keep My covenant, then you shall be a special treasure to Me above all people; for all the earth is Mine. `And you shall be to Me a kingdom of priests and a holy nation.' These are the words which you shall speak to the children of Israel,"" (Exod. 19:5-6). This is also stated scripturally as something which is *undefiled* or has *perfect purity.* Such a priesthood is set in order and is so by directives given from God to the church. They should be joined in unity and agreement as to how this mystical body operates.

Consider then the large disagreements in the church of God among denominations all through the world today? Schism is a result of sin. It has no place in the body. The church should be one; one in its members and service as a holy priesthood offering up that which the Father seeks as worshippers. Jesus said, "I pray that they may be all one," (John 17:21). Today, *they are not.* They should be one in knowledge, one in judgment and affection, one heart united to Christ by those sacred bonds of faith and love. Is it hard to see why the church is not so effective today with so many opinions and divisions, and such? Yet, how can the priests of this spiritual temple offer sacrifices without contending for the faith, resolving to follow God, separating from the world, giving thanks in all things, serving one another, being faithful, loving, noble, thoughtful, submissive, denying self and relying on God, sound in doctrine, eminently spiritual in their motivation, having godly affection one to another, consoling, encouraging, giving heartily for support of the church, in common fellowship in the Spirit, growing, and so unified in Christ through an obligated vow to uphold such truths? There is *no unity* without these things in any church.

Christian unity must be set within the context of understanding God's revealed will in Scripture, where they all have the same holy affections and love for the same holy principles God has given his holy nation. If they are not unified in this way, division gives way to practical hypocrisy. This is why unity in the mystical body of Christ is to be prayed for and to be labored for. "Can two walk together, unless they are agreed?" (Amos 3:3). To *walk together* in *unity* as a *holy nation*, not holy individuals, is a happy experience in walking together in the same path of truth and godliness. Whatever is contrary, then to truth and happiness in unity is not for Christ, but against him.

Reader, is your church unified in the Gospel as a holy priesthood *together?* The Westminster Divines said in their "Desires Concerning Unity and Conformity in Religion," there is, "nothing so powerful to divide the hearts of people as division in religion; nothing so strong to unite them as unity in religion."[17] You cannot even *hope* for unity unless there is a common agreement to it. What agreement can be had without *covenanting* together? It is impossible. They said, "...there can be small hope of unity in religion, which is the chief bond of peace and human society, unless first there be one form of ecclesiastical government."[18] Unity is founded on *doctrinal order.* There can be no unity in acceptable sacrifice without the exegesis that goes along with the word "acceptable." You have to know God's will, and God's word. No one is ever an island to themselves. No one can ever say it's just me and my bible. This is one of the reasons why historical theology is so important. What is the rule of faith? What has the church believed? What have they always taught? God has made it clearly apparent that there is often safety in good counsel together.

---

[17] Hetherington, W.M., *The History of the Westminster Assembly of Divines,* (Coconut Creek, FL: Puritan Publications, 2006) 257.
[18] Ibid.

Consider some directives on being unified as a church. As members of the mystical body you are to communicate with one another. How? In both domestic and sacred fellowship. You have domestic unity in taking counsel together. That means talking to people. In helping one another in support if needs be and opportunity allows. "To do good and to communicate forget not, for with such sacrifices God is well pleased," (Hebrews 13:15). This is done especially to *saints*. "As we have opportunity, let us do good unto all men, especially to them who are of the household of faith," (Galatians 6:10). It is done in fellowship together. This is what the early church did from house to house. "That they brake bread from house to house," (Acts 2:46).

You also have religious unity, both publicly and privately. In Public ordinances Christians are a holy priesthood. They have service in public ordinances, in the word, sacrament, and prayer. We see all these things come together in Acts 2:42, "They continued steadfastly in the Apostle's doctrine, and fellowship, and in breaking of bread, and in prayers," (Acts 2:42). In hearing the word; "they continued in the Apostle's doctrine;" that is, in hearing them preach, to which end they frequently went back to the temple, "They continued with one accord daily in the temple," (verse 46); why? *viz.* to hear the word. When you hear the word, you have unity if what is heard is also practiced. "They continued in the Apostle's doctrine, and in the fellowship of breaking bread, and in prayers." In the sacrament of the Lord's Supper. In praying together at stated prayer meetings. In *unity*. The point in that it was frequent, implied by the word continued, frequently meeting as the Lord allows, frequently together at the Lord's Table.

I don't understand churches that are not frequent in these things. They have the Lord's Supper once a quarter? Is that "frequently"? Frequently in doctrine and preaching. Frequently in prayer. Drawing near as Peter exhorts in *all these things*. The church says, "Come let us lift up our hearts with our hands unto God in the Heavens," (Lamentations 3:41). You see, they *come together*.

To this we also have the unified praising of Christ by God's directive of singing psalms, which as a divine institution, was not only used in the Old Testament, but prophesied concerning the Gentiles in the church in the New Testament. Not even so much unity as expressly stated by the Apostle Paul in Ephesians 5:19, Colossians 3:16, but prophesied in wonderful verses like, "Oh, give thanks to the LORD! Call upon His name; Make known His deeds among the peoples! Sing to Him, sing psalms to Him; Talk of all His wondrous works! Glory in His holy name; Let the hearts of those rejoice who seek the LORD!" (Psa. 105:1-3). This is done among Gentiles, *together*. During the time of the completion and work of the Messiah the Gentiles will come unified in worship.

All the spiritual metaphors Peter uses are *worship* related. They are not *willy nilly* by Peter, nor the Spirit, for that matter. They all have to do with worship: temple, sacrifice, holy priests, and the like. *Worship related*, having an eye to praise, all done in the spirit of unity.

As much as this kind of holy unity should exist, we must consider a note of hypocrisy, conspiracy and division. A *verbal unity* among those that do not hold Christ as their head, well, these are not really priests, nor part of the holy nation. It is just talk with them. People join a church to join a church. John Flavel said, "This is rather a conspiracy, than gospel-unity."[19] In such there is no spiritual unity; it is a facade. Spiritual unity is only possible in and through Christ, and in and through the Spirit sent from Christ with regenerate believers who are part of the royal holy priesthood. If people are void of it, they have no real unity in the mystical body though they might be members of the visible church. People like this in the church are merely hypocrites, who hold a club-mentality towards unity with the saints, and as all hypocrites do, and they *pretend* to belong to Christ. In point of fact, they have no real vitality in him. They do not sit on the Living Stone, they are not living stones, they are robbers. They have no real affections for the saints, and instead, they often raise divisions and commotions in it. Of these the apostle John says 1 John

---

[19] Flavel, John, *The Whole Works of John Flavel*, Volume 3, (London: Printed for W. Baynes and Sons, 1820) 595.

2:19. "They went out from us, but they were not of us; for if they had been of us, they would, no doubt, have continued with us; but they went out, that it might be made manifest that none of them were of us."

The unity of the saints as Christ's *Mystical Body* is founded on Christ the Living Stone. Stones not set on Christ are *not alive* and are *merely* stones. They are inanimate objects, dead to the core regardless of how ornamental they may look in the garden of the church. In Christ's spiritual building they are of no consequence.

Consider also, a brief note on main reasons for divisions in the church. There are many occasions for division in our day. From without – the devil bringing in false doctrine through false teachers. From within – non-essential principles that the church divides on which don't matter in the grand scheme of things. From odd practices – from emotional attachment to things that may not be of profit like what color the rug is in the sanctuary or how the landscaping looks in the front of the building. There can be no agreement, no growth, without uniformity in foundational matters, but how much is squabbled over on things that don't matter? Such sinful divisions hurt Christ's church. He commanded us that we are to love one another. In this way the universal rule is still the best: in essentials unity, in non-essentials liberty, in all things charity. Let us remember that the unity of the saints as Christ's Mystical Body is founded on him as the Living Stone which gives us life and vitality that we might render to God worship that is acceptable and holy.

Mark 2: Public Prayer

"Pray without ceasing," (1 Thess. 5:17).

"I exhort therefore, that, first of all, supplications, prayers, intercessions, and giving of thanks, be made for all men...I will therefore that men pray every where, lifting up holy hands, without wrath and doubting," *etc.*, (1 Tim. 2:1-8).

In this chapter we will consider two texts, 1 Thess. 5:17 and then 1 Timothy 2:1-8. There are, in these two texts, two exhortations; one to the church at Thessalonica, and one to Paul's apprenticed minister, Timothy.

The exhortation to the Thessalonian church is set amidst miscellaneous directives. It is more specifically set within the context of *Christ's immanent return*, and the manner in which Christians are to live every day in the end times, so to speak. They are to not be ignorant (verses 3-8). They are to house their wisdom and understanding in that Christ elected them for salvation (verses 9-10). They are to comfort one another (verse 11). They are urged to give due honor to those ministers among them as a corporate body (verses 12-13). Those ministering in the congregation (verses 14-15). They are to always be in a state of rejoicing (verse 16), and they are to always be in a state of praying (verse 17). They are to always be in a state of thanksgiving (verse 18). They are to always be sensitive to the Spirit's leading (verse 19). They are to hold fast to preaching, and God's truth held in preaching (verses 20-21). And, they are always to keep themselves safe from evil, even things with the appearance of evil (verse 22). All these spiritual sacrifices they do *as a church*.

They are exhorted (commanded) to pray without ceasing *as a church* (verse 17). This is an extremely easy verse to translate, since it is only comprised of two words. *Pray incessantly.*[1] Today, people use the phrase *without ceasing* more than they do the phrase *incessantly*, but the word *incessant* is a more literal rendering of the idea. It means they are to pray relentlessly and persistently. Now, it *cannot* mean that the Thessalonian church was to pray continuously doing nothing other than pray. This would be impossible. They must eat, sleep, hear the word preached, sing psalms, breathe, *etc.* What Paul is doing is reproving the general neglect of prayer in the church and setting forth a particular mindset. Prayer is not negotiable. Prayer is not to be sporadic (as if useful only sometimes). Prayer is like breathing to the congregation, it is to be done *incessantly*. It should be second nature to a Christian. The church is to have a continual attitude toward unified prayer. Remember, Paul wrote this *for the church*, which is also applied to the individual. It is, in fact, a necessary duty. It is a sanctifying duty.

---

[1] ἀδιαλείπτως προσεύχεσθε (1 Thess. 5:17).

Bear in mind, "...nothing is to be refused if it is received with thanksgiving; for it is sanctified by the word of God and prayer," (1 Tim. 4:4-5). Paul gives directives to his apprenticed minister in his letter of 1 Timothy. He writes it to Timothy, to the pastor of a church. He charges Timothy to pray for all men, with the men of the church, through Christ, in a manner of faithfulness and purity. "I desire therefore that the men pray everywhere, lifting up holy hands, without wrath and doubting," (1 Tim. 2:8). The Greek word *desire*, is really the word *purpose* combined with a *dash of hope*. Paul set in purpose what men ought to do together in the church in which Timothy is there to instruct. Everywhere, in *all the churches* planted by Paul, the men pray in lifting up pious, religious hands without anger or doubting. They are to *lift up their hands*. This is a Jewish connotation that is akin to vowing or swearing. That what they pray they swear to or make a vow of in a truthful manner. They are not to be overwhelmed by God's providences. They are to pray believing that what they pray, in accordance with the word of God, that God promises to bring it to pass. There is no room for doubt. Such is eminently pious and required.

Men are to pray in the church when the church gathers to pray. They pray in purity and faithfulness together. On this passage, Philip Doddridge called this a plea for "social prayer," in a section of lectures[2] on Christian virtue in the church. "Christians are to

---

[2] Lecture 143.

assemble together for the public worship of God, that thereby a solemn profession of religion may be made, that their affection to each other may be testified and cultivated, and that such instructions may be given as may tend to improve their minds in knowledge and holiness."[3] Paul shows Timothy that the men praying together, socially, amidst others, without ceasing, is a duty of Christian churches and should be led by the minister, Timothy. This is what the Apostle desired with hope, for all churches everywhere. That includes all churches, for all time, until the consummation of the ages.

Christ's church should be a house of incessant prayer in purity and faithfulness to God. *The 1647 Westminster Confession of Faith* 21:3 says, "Prayer with thanksgiving, being one special part of religious worship, is by God required of all men; and that it may be accepted, it is to be made in the name of the Son, by the help of his Spirit, according to his will, with understanding, reverence, humility, fervency, faith, love, and perseverance; and, if vocal, in a known tongue. Prayer is the soul breathing itself into the heart of its heavenly Father. It is taking the word of God, forming it into an argument, and retorting that back to God again. It is reminding God of his promises.

Now it is important to place that doctrine of prayer into the context of not only private devotions,

---

[3] Doddridge, Philip, *The Works of Philip Doddridge*, Volume 5, (London: Edward Baines, 1801) 291.

but prayer amidst the worship service where God dwells in the midst of his people, in the stated meeting of the church where the men pray lifting up holy hands. This does not exclude the women from the meeting. It merely exercises the stated duty of the men. Women are to pray silently along with the men as they pray outwardly. Such a support in this way is shown to the men, and such a duty is exercised in accordance with the Scriptures that give instructions to how women are to act as they attend the public worship of God. "Let a woman learn in silence with all submission. And I do not permit a woman to teach or to have authority over a man, but to be in silence," (1 Tim. 2:11-12). "And if they want to learn something, let them ask their own husbands at home; for it is shameful for women to speak in church," (1 Cor. 14:35). This is not a negative point, but rather, it's a covenantal point. It does not forbid *women singing*. But, it is not permitted for a woman to speak in church, by way of proposing questions, though under the desire to learn for her own pleasure; but rather, it is required that she should ask her husband at home (1 Corinthians 14:35). Why? 1 Peter 3:7, "Likewise ye husbands dwell with them according to knowledge," as a man of knowledge, that they may not only be able to know their own duty, but instruct their wives: "Let them ask their husbands at home," (1 Cor. 14:35; and he is called "the guide of her youth.") B.B. Warfield said, "That the injunction of speaking in the church to women is precise, absolute, and all-inclusive. They are to keep silent in the churches—and that means in all the public meetings for worship; they are not even to ask questions."[4] The reason for this, it encroaches on husbands and elders; it is a *covenantal* sin.

Public prayer has a biblical history throughout Scripture. Prayers are always seen in public worship in the Old Testament, and there are many Scriptures, but we will only look at a few. Solomon is said to publicly pray, "Then Solomon stood before the altar of the LORD in the presence of all the assembly of Israel, and spread out his hands toward heaven; and he said: "LORD God of Israel, there is no God in heaven above or on earth below like You, who keep Your covenant and mercy with Your servants who walk before You with all their hearts," (1 Kings 8:22-23). Ezra was said to pray at the evening sacrifice publicly. "At the evening sacrifice I arose from my fasting; and having torn my garment and my robe, I fell on my knees and spread out my hands to the LORD my God," (Ezra 9:5). Such public prayers were given by Solomon, Asa, Hezekiah, Ezra, Jehoshaphat, *etc.*

Public prayer also formed an important part of the service of the Jewish synagogue, which, from an early period, certainly from the time of Ezra, constituted the regular sabbatical worship of the church. The synagogue service was, in substance, the model of the Christian church. The titles and functions of the officers, and the

---

4   See   http://www.apuritansmind.com/pastors-study/paul-on-women-speaking-in-the-church-by-dr-benjamin-b-warfield/

form of worship, were the same. The Jewish place of worship was called, in Scripture, *the house of prayer.* Zechariah makes mention of it in 8:21, "Come let us go speak daily to pray before the Lord." Christians should think, *I will go also.* "Come, let us go..." The collective body going off to worship in prayer together.

Public prayer is also seen in the New Testament. The early church prayed together. "And they continued steadfastly in the apostles' doctrine and fellowship, in the breaking of bread, and in prayers," (Acts 2:42). This is a very simple concept. It is a very important concept. It is the collective body of Christ coming together in submission to God's sovereignty over them, to petition Christ's throne and yield to his providence in all things. "...but we will give ourselves continually to prayer," (Acts 6:4). If ministers pray together, the church should be praying together too. "And when he had said these things, he knelt down and prayed with them all," (Acts 20:36). *All,* not privately, but corporately. "When we had come to the end of those days, we departed and went on our way; and they all accompanied us, with wives and children, till we were out of the city. And we knelt down on the shore and prayed," (Acts 21:5). Here we find the constant attitude of prayer. The constant reliance on God in every providence. 1 Thess. 5:17 and 1 Tim. 2:8 cater also to this point for public prayer in the church.

In church prayer meetings the men are to pray in purity and faithfulness together. That doesn't exclude women praying silently in the prayer meeting as much as the congregation prays in the pastoral prayer. But the men are instructed to pray aloud together in a particular religious manner. The Lord Jesus saw God's temple...how?...as *a house of prayer.* God's house, his temple, is described as the house of prayer. ""It is written, 'My house is a house of prayer,' but you have made it a 'den of thieves.''" (Luke 19:46). When people make church something else other than a house of prayer they become thieves to God's intention for that place. Is it not interesting that God's house is not called a house of preaching or a house of doctrine? Prayer is set at a high priority in this way in the midst of the congregation. It teaches God's sovereign providence over willing Christians submitting themselves to his will.

What did people do at his house of prayer? They *prayed.* There his people met together to seek his face. Jesus explained God's house with this in mind, "Even them I will bring to My holy mountain, and make them joyful in My house of prayer. Their burnt offerings and their sacrifices will be accepted on My altar; For My house shall be called a house of prayer for all nations,'" (Isa. 56:7). The Jews should have never looked inwardly, but outwardly in trying to gather in as many from all nations to come together and share in submissive obedience to the providence and sovereignty of God. This Scripture in Isaiah, speaking of Gospel times, speaks of people coming together from all around the world in their respective and providentially placed geographic areas, to pray. Thomas Hooker said, "How can we come to the House of Prayer, and not be moved with the very glory of the place itself so to frame our affections praying, as does best beseem them whose suits the Almighty who there sits to hear, and his Angels attend to further? When this is ingrafted in the minds of men, there needed no penal statutes to draw them unto public prayer."[5] He is saying, when the Christian understands the importance of prayer, there is no need to give them a law to go do it. It's written with an iron pen on their new heart. It's a natural response to having a heart that beats after God. Christians pray and they do it together. They pray alone. They pray in little churches of their home. But they most desire to pray in big meeting houses at stated prayer meetings.

What does that say for those churches who, 1) don't have a prayer meeting (people just aren't interested in coming?), or 2) have only a little turnout from their congregation at prayer meetings. "It is written, 'My house shall be called a house of prayer,'" (Matt. 21:13). "Then He taught, saying to them, "Is it not written, 'My house shall be called a house of prayer for all nations'?" (Mark. 11:17). In this, Oliver Heywood said, "Public prayer in a congregation is where the body is seen and voice is heard,"[6] The *Christian* man shows up, and prays.

---

[5] Hooker, Richard, *The Works of Richard Hooker*, Volume 1, (London: B. Baines, 1825) 484.
[6] Heywood, Oliver, *The Works of Oliver Heywood*, Volume 3, (London: John Vint, 1825) 5.

Consider also 1 Cor. 11:1-19, which involve head coverings in public during prayer when the "woman prays", and Paul uses prayer as an argument. (My intention is not to get into head coverings here). "For first of all, when you come together *as a church*," (1 Cor. 11:18). "Every man praying or prophesying, having his head covered, dishonors his head. But every woman who prays or prophesies with her head uncovered dishonors her head, for that is one and the same as if her head were shaved," (1 Cor. 11:4-5). This concerns public prayer time. Paul is explaining head coverings in public prayer. *Social prayer* together in the house of prayer. He argues for holy submission and obedience to God. Now keep in mind, he is not making a distinction here about out loud or silent. The women pray in *silence* with the sign of submission over them.

Consider some of these quotes about the importance and exercise of the corporate prayer meeting, and also remember that whole books have been written on this subject. Thomas Ridgley said those who pray in public during public prayer times, "one is the mouth of the whole assembly."[7] Corporately, they come together, and that mouth praying prays on behalf of the people, and the people sit in agreement with him.

James Ussher said, "Public prayer is a prayer made of, and in the congregation, assembled for the service of God, (Psalm 84:1, *etc.*) "How lovely is Your

---

[7] Ridgley, Thomas, *The Works of Thomas Ridgley,* Volume 4, (Philadelphia, PA: W. Woodward, 1845) 93.

tabernacle, O LORD of hosts!'"" (Psa. 84:1). Loveliness adorns the house of prayer. They assemble in this beauty because God desires them in such stated meetings to glorify him in his attributes.[8]

Jonathan Edwards said, "The sacraments are ordinances; so this is true of public prayer...called the ordinance of God's house, or of public worship; and [is] intended in the doctrine: it is the profanation of these ordinances that is spoken of in the text: "They came into my sanctuary to profane it; and lo! thus have they done in the midst of mine house," saith God."[9] Prayer is an ordinance, a means of grace, which God has set down for the good of the people covenanted together in the church. It can be done badly, or it can be done in a holy manner. Fall asleep during prayer, and it's done badly. Pray in a way that is contrary to Scripture, and it's done badly. Pray just so others can hear, and it is done badly. Have wandering thoughts in prayer and its done badly. Pray in a manner consistent with God's directives and it will be a source of corporate blessing. The Spirit always seemed to baptize the people of God afresh with power while in unified corporate prayer (read the books of Acts). The general nature of this kind of corporate prayer, is an opening or making known of the desires of the heart collectively. Desire is the soul of prayer, and there must not only be habitual desires, but they must

---

[8] Ussher, James, *A Body of Divinity,* (London: R.B. Seeley, 1841) 457.
[9] Edwards, Jonathan, *The Works of Jonathan Edwards*, Volume 4, (New York, NY: Levitt and Allen, 1852) 66.

be vocalized and made real for the whole congregation to hear. Praying is the pouring out of congregation's souls in actual desires after the good things they lack or need. "With my soul I have desired You," (Isa. 26:9).

Thomas Gouge said, "The voice is not excluded, and is necessary in public prayer in the church ... it is used for stirring up our devotions, and keeping our minds from wandering thoughts, provided it is not done with an intention to be heard and taken notice of by others, which will argue gross hypocrisy."[10] Prayer in this way is a public calling on God. The church unites in their confession, thanksgiving and prayer as Christ's mystical body. God is not merely invoked by individuals, but by the whole body at one time. He is invoked in this way, corporate, for his glory, and for the benefits which then overflow onto the people when they act in this righteous manner. There is, annexed to Christ's words on discipline and governance in the church, added a special promise to prayers that are offered up publicly. "If two of you shall agree on earth as touching any thing that they shall ask, it shall be done for them of my Father which is in heaven. For where two or three are gathered together in my name, there am I in the midst of them."

Zacharias Ursinus rightly said, "Public prayer is that which, by the use of certain words, is offered up to God by the whole church in the congregation, the minister leading, as it is right and proper that he should

---

[10] Gouge, Thomas, *The Works of Thomas Gouge*, (London: E & E Hosford, 1811) 475.

in the public gatherings of the church. Language, or the use of the tongue, is necessary for this form of prayer."[11] One puritan preacher said, God gave you men a tongue, use it when you pray. Glorify God with all your body, not just part of it.

All neglect of God's worship and ordinances should be condemned, in not observing them in their practice. This includes the spiritual declension of not attending public prayer. Neglecting public prayer, in a place God calls his house, is offensive to him. "Have all the workers of iniquity no knowledge, Who eat up my people as they eat bread, And do not call on the LORD?" (Psa. 14:4). It's atheistical not only not to have a stated prayer meeting, but be averse to attending it and participating in it as a man (or woman) in the church. How do people hear such biblical directives and not bow before the Sovereign God who commands them to act and think in a very specific manner for his glory? The neglect of public prayer in the congregation is a sin that people are guilty of when they unnecessarily are absent from the public ordinances, or, through laziness or carelessness leave off which God calls them to do. They even neglect public prayer when they close their eyes during that time, but do not agree and pray along with what is being said. Those distracting wandering

---

[11] Ursinus, Zacharias, *The Commentary of Ursinus on the Catechism*, (Cincinnati, OH: Elsi Street Printing Company, 1851) 620.

thoughts in God's worship wreak havoc on such assemblies.

John Willison said, "Prayer is a principal part of God's worship, and therefore is frequently put for the whole, Zech. 8:21-22 and Acts 16:23. Therefore, God's temple of old was called the house of prayer. Public prayer is most necessary for averting judgements, obtaining blessings, and preserving love and unity among Christians; also, it is a solemn owning the God whom we serve in the face of the world, and so highly glorifies God."[12]

Richard Sibbes said, "I could wish that men would be more in public prayer,"[13] You see, prayer has a very large promise attached to it. It has a *large* promise; Matt. 7:7, "Ask, and it shall be given you; seek, and ye shall find; knock, and it shall be opened unto you." Would not the congregation do well to ask, seek and knock collectively? Jesus was, here in that text, speaking to the officers of his church in his sermon on the mount.

Thomas Boston exhorted, "[Prayer] is called seeking of God, and is the highway to find him, and it has been the gate of heaven to many a soul. It is a four-leaved gate, and at every one of the leaves the King has shown himself to poor sinners. Public prayer is the place at which Lydia got her heart opened where prayer was

---

[12] John Willison, *The Practical Works of John Willison*, Volume 4, (London: John Pillans and Son, 1816) 98.
[13] Sibbes, Richard, *The Works of Richard Sibbes*, Volume 7, (London: James Nisbet, 1864) 73.

customarily made," (Acts 16:13).[14] It should be repeated, and exhorted, Christ saw his church as a place of prayer. "My house is a house of prayer," (Luke 19:46).

Nathaniel Vincent said, "In the sanctuary of the church the Lord promises something to his people where it is not found elsewhere...for the united prayers of many saints together are stronger and more apt to prevail. How sharply are those to be reproved, who instead of praying with all prayer, use no prayer, but live in the almost total neglect of this duty."[15] We call such people who neglect it *atheists.*

If Christ saw his house as a place of prayer, and his body is his mystical house in which he now dwells, should not the church see this house characterized as a house of corporate prayer? How shall they do this if they do not pray together?

Public prayer has been the norm forever in the church of Jesus Christ. Look back on any revival in church history and you find the Spirit of God being poured out in the midst of the church gathered together praying. We should love to pray, and learn to pray better. We should bear with one another in prayer, and long to hear the men pray in such a way as to usher the church before the throne of grace. Have you ever gone to a prayer meeting where the church was praying together

---

[14] Boston, Thomas, *The Whole Works of the Late Reverend Thomas Boston,* Volume 10, (Aberdeen: George and Robert King, 1851) 492.
[15] Vincent, Nathaniel, *The Spirit of Prayer*, (Coconut Creek, FL: Puritan Publications, 2013) 89.

and the Spirit of God fell on the people? Have you ever been in a place where the presence of God was so thick and heavy that it was almost tangible to you during public prayer? If you have, why would you not want to experience that every week, Lord willing? If you have not, why would you not seek a fresh baptism in the Spirit of power in such ordinances constantly? It is another place, another opportunity to praise God, and to be blessed by him as a church. Be reminded, though, that it is Christ's church, not your church, and you are to bend to the will of God in all these things.

What you like, what you think you have time for, what you think you want to be interested in or not, those are unimportant. Christ's directives for you his people, come first. We are to love his commandments, because for the Christian, for us as professing believers, his commandments are *not burdensome*. Pray without ceasing. Men, pray, lifting up holy hands. Maybe you have never thought about the church as a house of prayer. Well, here we are; Jesus died so you can have access to God and pray in his house. We've been instructed by Paul, Christ, God, by ministers through the history of the church in revivalist setting, and normative settings, and see that public prayer is something Christians engage in, as they do doctrine, fellowship and the sacraments as a church. They have done this for hundreds, no, thousands of years. It could be that people don't like others in the church and so you don't want to be with them in prayer; I'm sure some churches have that problem where not everyone gets along. That doesn't negate the command. In Luke 18:10, even in public prayer, the Pharisee stood next to the tax collector. The Pharisees even prayed out loud for the tax collector to hear him. Now we don't do that in a negative or hurtful way, but consider, even these two people who didn't much like each other, went to the temple to pray publicly, and stood together to do so, anyway. God's house is a house of prayer, for both the penitent, and even hypocrites.

Public Prayer is not only clearly seen, but it is clearly commanded that you pray, if you are a man in any congregation. How could you at any time, neglect that duty? It may be you are sick, or some frowning providence hinders you from coming at some point in time. But all things considered, if we know what God desires of us and we don't want to take time to do it, what does that say about our profession? Consider, providentially, blessed providences occur when the church prays together. Isn't it a wonderful thing for those of you who keep some kind of record of your personal prayers that see when God answers them? Don't you get excited about when personal prayers are answered in that way? How much more when the congregation sees God's movements in the body of the church before their very eyes. Prayer can be eminently exciting. Maybe you pray for a brother to make a right decision, seeing that he made a wrong decision about an important life occurrence? Then you come to see, not some little time later, God working to change the whole outcome. God has many things to move around. His decrees are attached to the prayers of the congregation, and *vice versa*. What if, then, you collectively have the men praying lifting up holy hands in every church across the nation, across the world, O my, what providences would we see? I would say we would first see an outpouring of penitence, and sanctification would soon occur. Great biblical, religious piety would ensue. Then, could it be that we would see an outpouring of revival? The world would change. The very world would indeed *change*.

Why would you not want to pray? Why are so many churches filled with people on Sunday morning, hardly a quarter come back on Sunday evening, and even less, a handful come back on Wednesday night to pray? Why? Because the Evangelical church is filled with *hypocrites*. They have their dash of religion and have other things to do. Want to find out in any church where the Christians are? Go to a prayer meeting. And if there is no prayer meeting, it's not a *Christian* church, for "My house WILL BE called a house of prayer." Here Christ sees prayer being taken for the whole worship of God.

Prayer meetings allow you to see your beloved brethren midweek or so for godly interaction and wholesome conversation. Prayer meetings can encourage you when you are discouraged. Prayer meetings encourage the Spirit's work to empower the people of God for service as a body. Prayer meetings can create more devotion to the church as a whole. Prayer meetings are sources of great spiritual blessings to the people, or even some new work that may be given to them for the good of the body.

Promises are attached to prayer meetings for your good. Public prayer is useful as God has promised special blessings in connection with it. "Call to Me, and I will answer you, and show you great and mighty things, which you do not know,'" (Jer. 33:3). Ask, seek knock, and it will be opened, for, "if My people who are called by My name will humble themselves, and pray and seek My face, and turn from their wicked ways, then I will hear from heaven, and will forgive their sin and heal their land," (2 Chron. 7:14). Not, if you all *individually* come; no, he says, *all my people.*

I have for you an exhorting note considering obstacles to overcome in public prayer meetings. This runs off the importance of sin in the camp. "But the children of Israel committed a trespass regarding the accursed things, for Achan the son of Carmi, the son of Zabdi, the son of Zerah, of the tribe of Judah, took of the accursed things; so the anger of the LORD burned against the children of Israel," (Joshua 7:1). The collective whole will suffer in public prayer at any one of these obstacles. Thomas Manton said, "A Christian is still to take heed that his access to God be not spoiled; either broken off, or carried on carelessly and formally. God will stand at a distance from us, or the heart will stand at a distance from God; God is provoked to withdraw by our disorderly walking; or else the heart will grow shy of God as Adam hid himself when he had sinned. If we give way to pride, and passion, and lust, and worldly-mindedness, how shall we pray, and look God in the face with any confidence?"[16] There are, then, seven obstacles to avoid in public prayer.

The obstacle of sin. You cannot walk contrary to God and his word and then expect him to listen to you. Blessings are attached to this ordinance and they are stifled by sin.

The obstacle of insincerity. One does not have faith exercised in the right way to pray something he does not believe will come to pass. This could also be called an obstacle of hypocrisy.

The obstacle of prideful prayers. These are often long. It is when people pray to be heard not by God but by others.

The obstacle of preaching instead of praying. These men do not pray, but preach little sermons. They tell the Lord all the things they do, and how they are done by them and they fail to pray to ask God for what the congregation needs.

The obstacle of confusion. What should I pray for? Prayer-meetings are often hindered by a lack of directness to God.

---

[16] Manton, Thomas, *The Works of Thomas Manton*, Volume 15 (London: James Nisbet and Co., 1873), 300.

The obstacle of being lukewarm. Cold prayers always freeze before they get to heaven. Christ does not want his people luke-warm, or cold, but on fire. *Zealous*.

The obstacle of neglecting the constituted means. A person prays, but they don't use the constituted means by which their prayer might be answered. They just wait for God to "answer prayer" without doing anything. They pray for a job, but they are not looking for a job. You pray for something, but do not act to *get* the something.

What means will God use in his church which is greater than God's use *of you* in this act of corporate prayer?

Mark 3: Tithing and Support

"And blessed be the most high God, which hath delivered thine enemies into thy hand. And he gave him tithes of all," (Gen. 14:20).

Contrary to popular belief, tithing is not about giving. Tithing is not about purposing in your heart what *you will give* the church. Tithing is part of a subdivision in the mortification of sin. It is primarily done in light of the fall. It is principally in contrast to the temporary nature of the present world. It is not mainly about *getting* a blessing, although certain tangible benefits arise from this eminently spiritual duty. It is sorely mistaken by a great number of professing Christians.

Tithing answers the question – what are you looking for? It answers the question – how much do you want it? I'll explain both of these in light of the life of Abram.

Melchizedek the priest comes to greet Abram in Genesis 14:18-20. Lot was taken captive, and an informant told Abram of the circumstance. Abram looks to rescue his kinsman from the attacking kings, and is victorious in gaining his family back. When he returns he is met with the mysterious figure Melchizedek. Melchizedek's name is the "King of Righteousness" (or *king of justice*). In Hebrew it means "my king is sedeq," my king is justice. His name comes from "Salaym" a short version of "Yerusalaym", *Jerusalem,* which means "city of peace." This Melchizedek visits Abram and brings out bread and wine and they partake of it. Think this through, *bread and wine,* in a solemn communion with God. After they eat and drink, Melchizedek blesses Abram, "El Elyon, God Most High," in this way, God blesses him. The Hebrew concept of *blessing* means "covenantally to endue with power, prosperity and longevity." In turn, they bless God, "Give glory to God," or in essence, "praise God for who He is." In this they "called on His name."

God has won the victory in a dire circumstance, and so Abram *naturally* (memorize that word) tithes a tenth of the plunder from his victory, a tenth of his estate, to Melchizedek. Hold your thoughts for a moment on the tithe he gave.

Now this visit by Melchizedek was to confirm God's covenant with Abram, as Melchizedek was the *type* of both the person and office of Jesus Christ as the book of Hebrews so excellently portrays. What did Melchizedek do? He blessed Abram with both spiritual and temporary blessings being the typological mediator of the Most High God. He showed Abram that he has received from God in covenant a blessing of righteousness and peace. We see, not long after this, that Abram's faith is shown as the archetype, as the standard of believing faith, as the epistles of Romans and Galatians demonstrate. It is in this kind of faith that *Abraham* is called a friend of God, and has given to him the imputed righteousness of God. *God* himself is his exceedingly gracious reward. *God* is his shield.

This Melchizedek was the type of Christ to come, confirming to Abram the eternal joy in saving grace that *Abraham* ultimately received of God. Though Abram, at this point in time, was looking at a physical man, the person of Melchizedek, he was seeing the spiritual representation of Jesus Christ as a shadow, as a type, and was blessed by God's covenant in him. Melchizedek, pre-figured the eternal One. Who is this Melchizedek?

Melchizedek appears suddenly, gives a blessing, and then disappears just as quickly. There is no more mention of him until David sings of him in Psalm 110, "You are a priest forever in the order of Melchizedek." This psalm teaches aspects of the Covenant of Redemption. It speaks of the priestly work of Yeshua, the Savior, the Anointed One to save his people. This psalm, though, gives us no more information than what Genesis 14 gives us. But it does gives us a little more application of what Melchizedek means in Scripture, it says "priest forever." What makes Melchizedek stand out in this Psalm is he is a priest forever, and he is a foreshadow of Christ. David sings about Christ and his office, of His kingship and priesthood. But then, there is no more information there. We must look to the New Testament that holds for us more information. Hebrews 7:1-3, "For this Melchizedek, king of Salem, priest of the Most High God, who met Abraham returning from the slaughter of the kings and blessed him, to whom Abraham gave a tenth part of all, first being translated "king of righteousness," and then also king of Salem, meaning "king of peace", without father, without mother, without genealogy, having neither beginning of days or end of life, but made like the Son of God, remains a priest forever." Verses 1-3 in the Greek are one long continuous sentence that gives us some insight into the character of Melchizedek. He is King of Salem, priest of the Most High God, blessed Abram, was tithed to by Abram, his name means *king of righteousness and peace*, without father, without mother, without genealogy, having neither beginning or ending of days, being *like* the Son of God, and because of this his priestly line remains continually. This is all *comparatively.* Some believe, wrongly, that Melchizedek is the pre-incarnate Christ. Hebrews does not make that connection, but rather makes a comparative connection based on the priestly work of this man, and the fulfillment of Christ's work in the line of Melchizedek.

The new information in Hebrews shows us two things: Melchizedek is a foreshadow or type of Christ, and Abram *saw him* as a type. But the writer in Hebrews in expounding this passage presses the reader to consider, what will Christian's do with the *fulfillment* of the type? Abram did something very specific with Melchizedek *as* a type. What will Christians do with the fulfillment of the type in Christ *who came already* – the rhetorical question and answer is, *they will do more; yes, they will do more than Abram did.*

Melchizedek is like Christ in that he has no genealogy in a *book of Genealogies*, which foreshadows an eternal aspect of his priesthood. Christ is the eternal logos. Christ is God. Christ is the Alpha and Omega, the beginning and the end; he is the same yesterday, today and forever. It means God has established this priestly order forever. This order is different from the Levites, different from Zadok, different from any other; this priesthood alone has the power of eternity behind it. Even while they were in the loins of Abram, the writer of Hebrews says the Levites paid *tithes* to Melchizedek. *Before* there was a law there were *tithes*. There were tenths given to God. It was not commanded. Where do you find the command to give a tenth in Genesis? Rather, there is the pattern and the precept in the example. Why would Abram tithe? Hold *that* thought for a moment.

Melchizedek, foreshadowing Christ's priesthood, makes this order of priests eternal. Not eternal in being but eternal in *purpose and order* according to God's covenant. Melchizedek is not literally Christ – he is priest and king over a city. He is "like" Christ, and so the thing signified cannot be the thing and the thing signified at the same time. This is likened to the Lord's Supper. The supper represents Christ, and yet, it is not Christ himself physically. There is a *spiritual* connection. Melchizedek affirms the spiritual connection Abram has with the covenant blessing of Christ in the covenant of grace. All of this is a further confirmation of the Covenant of Grace to God's friend, Abram.

Abram communed with Melchizedek. Abram ate with Melchizedek bread and wine. Is this not a clear type of the Lord's Supper to come? They fellowshipped together around bread and wine. Then, a most interesting event occurred. Abram tithed to Melchizedek. *What* did he tithe? Abram gave him a tenth part of *all* he had. A tenth part assumes gross, not net. A tenth part of all, his entire estate. In many Hebrew and Syriac manuscripts the term is "tithe and first-fruits of all," of *everything*. But, *why* did he tithe? Why did he give a tenth? He tithed in a threefold manner to the situation: first, in response to blessing, where he regarded both the providence of God and blessing of God. God's providence gave him victory in rescuing lot. God's covenant renewal or confirmation is in and of itself enough to give such a submissive response.

Second, he has God. What is a tenth of temporary blessings in comparison to his exceedingly great reward of having God in covenant as friend? What does he do in response to worship, as an act of humility before God? Abram *worships*. There must be some natural response which is elicited through God's blessing. Natural as in the sense of outwardly flowing without hindrance, not natural as in opposite to supernatural. Natural as in *naturally*. This is in accordance with the kind of character Abram has. If he was a Christian in this way, he naturally would do this. He also does this as an act due to God's priest. There is something where he knows Melchizedek is *owed* in this way, being a representative of God's covenant. Abram has been very thoughtful in this way about God's covenant.

Third, there is a demonstration of his weaning from the world. He looked to the city made without hands. It directly connects Abram with dying to this fallen world; die to the world, grow in fellowship with God. These confirmations to Abram are of the grace found in the Covenant of Grace. That which God blessed him with through Melchizedek. Abram naturally in turn responds with humility and thanksgiving.

The doctrine to understand here is that Jesus Christ's priesthood is eternal and all his servants recognize that Lordship in their *natural* spiritual response. Melchizedek's priesthood is an example of the eternal priesthood in Christ, a Priest of Melchizedek, not Aaron or Zadok. Hebrews 7:26-26, "Therefore he is also able to save to the uttermost those who come to God through Him, since he always lives to make intercession for them. For such a high priest was fitting for us, who is holy, innocent, undefiled, separate from sinners, and has become higher than the heavens."[1] Psalm 110 in this way relates completely to Jesus Christ. It represents him in his glorious offices as prophet, priest and king. As a Prophet, he gathers the nations by the

---

[1] See Psalm 110.

proclamations of his gospel, the rod of his strength, verses 2-3. As the great High Priest of his people, shadowed in Melchizedek, verse 4, he is the one who brings people into fellowship with God through sacrifice and suffering. Yet, he is also the exalted, victorious, and governing King, verses 2-3, 5-6. This psalm ought to cause God's people to consider Christ's humiliation, and his exaltation. It shows how their minds must be set on the glorious Redeemer whose ministry is eternal. He has, by his own will and the joy set before him, purged his people's sins, and been exalted by God to the right hand of power. All those who trust in him alone may be saved.

Melchizedek is the greatest earthly priest that ever existed. He came to bless the lesser, and show Abram by his very presence, a shadow of Christ, and a slice of eternity. He comes upon the scene mysteriously and leaves it mysteriously. He comes to bless Abram by way of covenant. Abram realizes his lesser status; the greatest patriarch, the greatest man in the world up to this point in time, realizes his *lesser* status. We see superiors and inferiors interacting as God has laid them out for specific purposes. He communes in the privilege, fellowships in the privilege, of this covenant confirmation, and tithes to Melchizedek. Why? Because Melchizedek's priestly lines hold the power of Messianic fulfillment – the heavenly city and the God of the heavenly city, Jesus Christ, the Covenant of Grace in Christ are bound up, wrapped up, veiled, foreshadowed, in Melchizedek. So, what is a *natural response* to this covenant communion by God's servant? It is a weaning away from the world.

Most times of weaning come through some kind of affliction. In this case, it is giving up of a bit of Abram's goods. Specifically, a tenth. John Owen said, "There can be no greater pledge nor evidence of divine love in affliction than this, that God designs by afflictions to make us partakers of his holiness, to bring us nearer to him, and make us more like him."[2] This occurs by weaning from the world and love to the world, whose vanity Christians openly discover and in their unsatisfied state with it, they break the association of love that is between it and their souls. This is breaking away from the world one step at a time, one week at a time. In this Christians are called to believe God by faith and contemplation of things which are more glorious and excellent, in which they may find rest and peace.

Subjection is affliction. Submission is affliction. Obedience is a kind of affliction of soul. Christians are often thoroughly afflicted to give up their finances for the kingdom. It is often because they fail to realize the covenant transaction taking place. Covenant confirmations are being made for their eternal well-being. What will their submissive response be to this? Consider that even the basics of the ministry of the church would never be able to continue if there were not

---

[2] Owen, John, (1616-1683). *An Exposition of the Epistle to the Hebrews*, Volume 4, (Edinburgh: Banner of Truth Trust, 1998) 587.

some obligatory part to uphold it financially by the communion of believers. The ministry of the Gospel is more important than worldly gain and worldly possessions. The realignment or focus of the Christian in this way centers on the propagation of the Gospel. How important is the ministry of the Gospel to the church? Ask, then, how the church tithes, or not. How important was the ministry of the Gospel to Abram? How important did *he* think that was? It was important enough to tap into his entire estate and give a tenth to support Melchizedek in the covenant blessings he received. Look at the reciprocal nature of fellowship here between Melchizedek the priest and Abram the believer; between the believer and Christ. Tithing is a communing with Christ, and the natural response of Christ's blessing from a believing heart; it houses in it mortification of the flesh, and a weaning away from the world. Here, this dying to the world is shown by Abram in his tithe; a tithe of all he had. Chrysostom said, "Humility is the foundation of Christian virtue."[3] Humility is set in the natural response of being weaned away from the world, to cling to the city whose maker and builder is God. The humble Christian puts to death the deeds of the body and in sanctification, is weaned from the world by the Spirit of Grace. Tithing will do that. Tithing *shows* that. It's a material substance that holds value to people. Does money not hold value to you?

---

[3] Mead, Matthew, *The Christian's Duty to Walk Wisely*, (Coconut Creek, FL: Puritan Publications, 2015) 64.

Is not the love of money opposite to the weaning and mortification that ought to occur in the life of a believer? Matthew Mead said, "Where the grace of God takes hold of the soul, it makes it as a weaned child, to all worldly things."[4]

Do Christians see tithing as a weaning from the world? I would argue they've not even considered it as such. They see it, like John Owen did, as *some kind of law*. We will see what that means in a moment.

They think tithing is just another thing God requires them to do. Give up their time. Give up their finances. Give up and trust God. Such things are very hard to do. The world has a very strong pull on things that hit hardest and closest to home for the Christian in their finances.

Weaning is spiritually followed by growth and strength. Find a professing Christian not growing in Jesus Christ, and it's true that he is still attached to the world in ways he might not even see. Find a Christian not growing and the world in some way has busied him and attracted him away from the invisible realities he should be holding onto. Where is that city made without hands for such a one? There are commitments to be made to Jesus Christ by those who profess allegiance to him and his eternal priesthood. Not to mention the fact that *Christ is God.* All this, which makes religion the business of the Christian, takes

---

[4] Mead, Matthew, *The Christian's Duty to Walk Wisely*, (Coconut Creek, FL: Puritan Publications, 2015) 65.

center stage as a natural response to communion with God in the act of tithing.

One would have thought a natural response to God's covenant was praying, or reading the bible, or meditating on the word; and those things certainly can be seen in that way. But they wouldn't have thought it was tithing. Tithing involves Christians in the expansion and propagation of the Gospel in the world; it refocuses their sight to the celestial city.

Abram has the shadow of Melchizedek's eternal priestly Messiah standing before him. Melchizedek was physically standing there. In response, Abram committed to physically offer up those things fitting for such a communion. That does not mean spiritual things were not important. Tithing is eminently spiritual. He didn't need to pray at that point, or meditate on the word, because the physical presentation of blessing was in front of his very eyes. It was within grasp of his very touch. Commitments to Jesus Christ, however, by those who are spiritually connected to him, are all spiritual in nature until the consummation of glory. Christian's don't have Christ standing physically before them, instead, they have the representations of spiritual duties to contend with until they go to heaven; that is the church, ministers and such. That means they pray, read the bible, study, meditate on the word, attend worship, partake of the sacraments, do good works, fast and they expand the kingdom of God through their natural worshipful response of covenant blessings in *tithing*.

These are spiritual acts of worship. There is no law against such things; and in Abram's life, there was no law for them; he just did them. Abram is a very sticky wicket for people who don't like the idea of tithing in the church. Nonetheless, these are all spiritual commitments to Jesus Christ. This was all before the law, priests, temples, *etc.* All Christians are obligated to spiritual acts of worship in this way.

Do all have the faith of father *Abraham?* Abram sees the eternal in Melchizedek who foreshadows Christ who holds the power to cancel sin and death and bring him to heaven. What do I do in response to such a confirming covenant blessing – Abram says, here is a tenth of all – *I tithe.* Everything about Melchizedek speaks to Abram in terms of the greatness of eternal things over the king of Sodom who was only interested in materialism. Abram says, I won't give you anything, King of Sodom, but I will confirm the blessing by giving everything including material possessions to Melchizedek. I want to be weaned from the world. I want the full covenant blessing; I want as much of heaven now as I can get, having my eyes fixed there, looking for Christ. Jesus fulfills, then, everything that is prophesied about in his work and sacrifice in the eternal priestly line of Melchizedek. Christians, now, ought to look to offer spiritual sacrifices to Christ in the same way Abram did.

The second doctrine to consider is that the tithe is an outward expression of dying to the world and demonstrating to God submission to his covenant blessings. One of the greatest proponents against the tithe as a law, under the Mosaic law, or further expounded by the Gospel, was John Owen. He said, "The precise law of tithing is not confirmed in the Gospel."[5] He's right. Tithing is not *a law* for the believer given in the codex of Christian duties in the New Testament. At that point many Christians give a sigh of relief. They do not want to be *obligated* to give up their money by some law. They have other things they would rather use their money for. They want to support small businesses, large businesses, order online, go out to eat, pay for popcorn at the movies and such things. I'm not saying those are bad, but is that the natural response of the Christian to tithing, *a sigh of relief?*

Listen to Owen continue as he wrestles this to the ground. "By the light of nature, all rules of reason and positive institutions, a portion of what God is pleased to give unto every man is to be returned unto him, in the way of his worship and service, wherein it may be used according unto his appointment; and whereas before the giving of the law, sundry holy men fixed on the tenth part, as that which was best to be so dedicated unto God...it is the best direction that can be given unto any what proportion of their estate should be set apart to this purpose."[6] Owen says, it's not a law, *it's the natural*

---

[5] Owen, John, *An Exposition of the Epistle to the Hebrews,* Volume 3, (Edinburgh: Banner of Truth Trust, 1998) 431.
[6] Ibid, 431.

response of people who claim to be Christian. Christians are to *still give a tenth portion* because the light of *Christian nature* teaches them it is so. Christ saw tithing as morally obligatory, "But woe to you Pharisees! For you tithe mint and rue and all manner of herbs, and pass by justice and the love of God. These you ought to have done," (Luke 11:42). In the fulfillment of things lawful, *you do this.* In the fulfillment of things Christian you are bound to do this as a natural response – provided you are really converted, and have the things of God in mind.

Yet, it is far more than the light of nature for a spiritual and material sacrifice of affliction for Christians. It is the natural response of the faithful Christian. This natural response sees and acknowledges God's blessing. It responds in thankfulness to him. It sees and responds to covenant blessings, which include God providing for them.

Why is the tithe (a tenth of all) an outward expression of affliction? It is dying to the world. It literally *costs Christians something.* Salvation for men cost God something – it cost him the life of his dear Son, his only Son, his perfect Son, Jesus Christ. Yes, we even see this typified in Abraham's directive, "Abraham, bring your son, your only son Isaac whom you love," and sacrifice him to me. God stopped faithful Abraham there on the mountain, but he sacrificed his own Son, Jesus Christ. God withheld nothing. What do you withhold from him?

Abram was not acting under a law of tithing. It was, however, a natural spiritual response to God's covenant blessing. At that point, the matter is theologically over on any debate of whether one should tithe or not. Is the Christian blessed? Then the response is warranted. Further implications, past that tenth, the natural response of a portion given back to God as spiritual worship, is also *cheerful giving.* More than a tenth. Before the Gospel, Abram gave a tenth. He did so in types and shadows. What will Christians do now that Christ has *come?* Christians often don't understand this. Statistically, and to their utter shame, they often "give" less. As it stands, based on Barna polls and such, only 5% tithe anything. The most they tithe is 3% (and keep in mind most polls are quite useless, so take those amounts with a grain of salt). Cheerful giving as the Apostle Paul outlines is giving extra, above and beyond that which is natural, as God so blesses the Christian, so he in turn blesses further than what is his basic natural response to God's blessing. In the collections and needs of Jerusalem, Paul said, "So let each one give as he purposes in his heart, not grudgingly or of necessity; for God loves a cheerful giver. And God is able to make all grace abound toward you, that you, always having all sufficiency in all things, may have an abundance for every good work," (2 Cor. 9:7-8). This is *past* the natural response or obligation of the thankful Christian. Simeon Ashe in his work, *Real Thankfulness* gives a demonstration of thankfulness to God as seen in Abram tithing; thankful for covenant blessings.[7]

Christ works on the soul to wean it from the world. The Hebrew idea behind *wean*, is to ripen, to deal fully with. The Christian is to be ripened away from the world. "Do not love the world or the things in the world. If anyone loves the world, the love of the Father is not in him," (1 John 2:15). Such dying to the world is expressed in Scripture by various terms: a resurrection to life, a quickening, a new creation, the new man, growth in the inward man, a dying to the world. It is a putting off the old man, the principles and passions, the corrupt notions and affections which we derive from Adam, to devote ourselves to God, to live to Christ, to walk in newness of life. Or how about this one: *and he gave him a tenth of all.* "But God forbid that I should boast except in the cross of our Lord Jesus Christ, by whom the world has been crucified to me, and I to the world." (Gal. 6:14). Tithing is a direct manifestation of the death of the Christian to the world in light of the death of Christ. This places tithing in a whole new light. It is much more than simply giving; consider Christ and consider *giving extra.* It has attached to it eternal, and covenantal ideas. It has attached to it the eternal sacrifice of Christ. It has attached to it the translation of a person from one world to another, from the dominion of darkness to the kingdom of light.

---

[7] Ashe, Simeon, *Real Thankfulness*, (Crossville, TN: Puritan Publications, 2016) 12.

Where is the Christian looking? Is he looking with father Abraham to the celestial city? Spiritual commitments to the eternal ruling and reigning Christ are to be made by diligent Christians. There are a number of spiritual duties that Christians regularly think about – prayer, bible reading, church worship and such, as spiritual sacrifices. Things not often thought about are fasting, as when Jesus said, "when you fast." Participating in the Lord's Supper through personal examination. Improving one's Baptism and joining in covenant blessings. Stewardship with supporting church through tithing and giving. Spiritual usefulness with gifts God has bestowed upon the Christian. Have you really thought about these things?

What is your natural response in thankful adoration to God? What are you looking for? With Abram, hopefully, you are looking for the city whose builder and maker is God. "He waited for the city which has foundations, whose builder and maker is God," (Heb. 11:10). How much do you want that? The natural response to seeking first the Kingdom of Heaven, is to die to the world. It is the mortification of sin. This means evaluating what you have in this world, and giving a tenth portion of that back to God. Then after that, cheerfully giving what you have purposed in your heart further than what is expected. Even from the beginning, it was a tithe of money, of that which cost Abram his livelihood.

Shall you serve God with things that cost you nothing? How thankful are you to God and how much do you desire to see God's kingdom ushered in? Really, think it through, and think well on it. Are you thankful for all those covenant blessings in Yeshua Messiah? Or are you stoic? Do you just bite your upper lip and sign the check over to the church with a wince? Or are you truly thankful for covenant blessings? It is a "put your money where your mouth is" type of service. Don't make your professing talk cheap in this light. Give of your livelihood, for God sees your heart. God will try your faith in giving; in that accommodating language, God wants to know how serious you are in your Christian walk. Christians are to look for a city whose builder is God and they die to the world. This place is not their home. They are merely sojourners here on earth. Tithing, or not, shows that heart-response.

Tithing propagates the Gospel ministry. How can a person say he loves Christ in sincerity, when he causes the church and its ministers and members to lack necessities? Rich people often have their hearts hardened and their inward spiritual disposition shut up. "Assuredly, I say to you that it is hard for a rich man to enter the kingdom of heaven," (Matt. 19:23). Those who remain uncharitable in this way according to Scripture are biblically cursed in life and in death; God will give them more money, will drown them in their money, will give them the *Midas* touch where everything turns to gold for them, and yet, in the end, they take not one penny with them to judgment. Not only are your afflictions cursed if you are like this, but your blessings are a curse as well. Malachi 2:2, "to curse their every blessing." Though you enjoy abundance of this world's goods, yet so long as you are hard hearted in this natural response of the believer, the curse of God is on you. They are cursed into eternity. James 2:13, "He shall have judgment without mercy, that hath shewed no mercy." James says that such material wealth will witness against them into eternity while they see, just out of grasp, all they had while in torment in hell. A lack of tithing curses men? A heart that is set on stinginess, and does not hold itself in the way of being liberal in giving, shows a deeper heart problem. Liberality was so well accepted in tithing in this way in the first four hundred years of the church after Christ, that their liberality toward the church and its ministers and the Gospel was so great, they far exceeded the tenth. Increase Mather said, "There is something due to God out of every man's estate, and the tenth of his incomes is the least that may be supposed."[8]

David Calderwood said, "The tenth was God's due, and he was pleased by a positive law to appoint that what should otherwise have been given to Him, should be bestowed on those his ministers."[9]

---

[8] Mather, Increase, A Discourse Concerning the Maintenance Due to Those that Preach the Gospel, (Boston, MA: B. Green, 1706) 39.
[9] Ibid, 50.

Ursinus in his catechism said this act surrounds the "heart of gratitude."[10]

Joseph Mede said, this is a "tribute of our Thanksgiving, whereby we acknowledge we are God's Tenants,"[11] in this world. It's not law, he says, its obligation, the natural response of the Christian to God.

Edward Leigh said, "The question should not be, whether tithes are due to the ministers of the Gospel, meaning as a duty of the people unto them, but rather whether they be not due unto God; for so is the style of the Scripture, all the tithes are mine as God says."[12]

Tithing supports the church and propagates the Gospel. It is a means to more of the Kingdom of heaven in the world. It is dying to the world, and disseminating the Gospel. In 1 Corinthians 9 Paul explains that ministers receive wages. Where do these come from? How shall they receive sustenance? Are they to wait for the ravens to feed them? Robert Cleaver said, "Can you defraud the minister in such a way?"[13]

How shall the poor in the church be provided for? If it is non-obligatory, and everyone simply purposes to give a little, a smaller percent, a smaller portion, in an instant the Gospel ministry could come tumbling down,

---

[10] Ursinus, Zacharius, *The Commentary of Ursinus on the Heidelberg Catechism*, (Cincinnati OH: T.P. Bucher, 1851) 571.

[11] Mede, Joseph, *The Works of Joseph Mede*, (London: Roger Norton, 1677) 171.

[12] Leigh, Edward, Of Pastors: of their Maintenance, *A System or Body of Divinity*, (London: A.M., 1654) 461.

[13] Dod, John, and Cleaver, Robert, *A Plain and Familiar Exposition of the Ten Commandments* (London: Richard Field, 1618) 238.

and there would be nothing for the poor, the widows and the orphans; which is part of what true religion is about as James teaches us.

The natural response of the Christian in the tithe supports the Gospel and the church. The cheerful response extends it even further in giving above and beyond. So, we find, Jesus Christ's priesthood is eternal and all his servants recognize that Lordship in their natural spiritual response. The tithe is an outward expression of dying to the world and demonstrating to God submission to his covenant blessings.

Mark 4: Gospel Worship

"And when He again brings the first-born into the world, He says, "And let all the angels of God worship Him,"" (Heb. 1:6).

This verse falls into the first part of this chapter in Hebrews as an argument for the utter supremacy of Jesus Christ over all of creation, and all created beings. I do not wish to get into ideas revolving around or in light of refuting Plato and his influence on the Greeks through certain aspects of Neo-Platonism, which hold certain arguments in this first chapter that color the intent of the author. My intention is to focus your attention on ideas revolving around this one verse, and truths in greater fulfillment compared to it.

In considering the supremacy of Jesus Christ, the writer first introduces the height of God's revelation to men. In times past he used mere men, moved by the Spirit, to bring his word. Now, he does this through the great exegete of the Son of Man who perfectly declares the Father to creation (the substance of John 1:18). He shows that this Savior is God's Son, incarnate, coequal and of the same substance of the Father and Spirit. He made the worlds. He is the brightness of the glory of God. He upholds all things as the Word Himself. He fulfilled the eternal covenant and sat down at the right hand of the power of God. In a more literal rendering of the verse, I translate this as, "when at that time He anew (again) brings the (*prototokos*) first born in among the inhabitants of the world, He says, "Let all the angels of God worship him." It may be that you see little difference in the way I've laid that out to you, than it is translated in your copy of Scripture. But I think what lacks in the translated versions we have is the relation of this verse to *time*. This verse is explicitly *time* related.

The only begotten Son of God has forever, outside the context of the created order, or of time itself, been the eternal Son, of the same substance of the Father and Spirit, of the same substance in power and glory. At a specific point in time, in the fullness of time, this eternal Son assumed to himself, in covenant with the Father through the power of the Spirit, a human nature to which the person of the Son was attached, and animated. At that particular time, this Son of God was introduced into the world in a particular manner. God incarnate, as a servant, willing to fulfill the eternal covenant of redemption for the glory of God, even unto death, came to work all the works of God in his flesh. In that covenant, he committed himself to the will of the Father, and in the unmatched power of the Spirit he redeemed in time his church, his bride, his peculiar people. He did this by his incarnation, his life, his death and his resurrection. The use of the term "again" or "anew" combined with "when" or "at that time" places the emphasis not solely on the Son as the only begotten of the Father who came as God incarnate, but now, again, as firstborn in something important, in whatever peculiar nature that is. What is he as first born?

Scripture uses the term *firstborn* in relation to the Son of God both as eternally generated, and as it depicts his resurrection and exalted or glorified state. "For whom he did foreknow, he also did predestinate to be conformed to the image of his Son, that he might be the firstborn among many brethren," (Rom. 8:29). "And he is the head of the body, the church: who is the beginning, the firstborn from the dead; that in all things he might have the preeminence," (Col. 1:18). "And from Jesus Christ, who is the faithful witness, and the first begotten of the dead, and the prince of the kings of the earth," (Rev. 1:5). And, so also, we have Hebrews 1:6 concerning his eternal nature and introduction in the flesh to the world. He is God's firstborn.

Keep in mind that first-born in this redemptive context, in this preeminent context of Hebrews 1, refers to his generation as the Son, but also has some connotations of the finality of his work in his resurrection because the angels are required to worship this eternally generated Son, now taken on flesh, and now come to heaven in glory. You see, it is not merely firstborn, but firstborn into the world due to covenant concepts. This eternal Son takes on human flesh in the world, accomplishes his work, and ascends to heaven in glory.

Whenever messengers of Christ use the term *resurrection* in light of the Gospel, it always has in it the fullness of the Gospel assumed. Covenant, incarnation, life, merit, works, the law of God, salvation, redemption, ransom, his infinite atonement, death, wrath, hell, the tomb, and such, which culminate in the stamp of approval of God's elect servant, the Christ in his resurrection, to all of this. Hebrews 1:6, however, quotes and demonstrates a Messianic fulfillment of something that is added to this idea of Christ being in the world, it is found that he is also firstborn from among the dead. And in this work in the world, the writer adds something to this as an argument or proof of Christ's eminent status in the redemptive plan of God, quoting Psalm 97:7, pertaining to worship. Yes, the passage we have read is a quotation from the Psalms. The eternally generated Son, clothed in human flesh, introduced to the world, is worshipped in his natural state by the angelic host. "Let all be put to shame who serve carved images, who boast of idols. Worship Him, all you gods," (Psa. 97:7). In the various places where men confound worship, they choose rather to serve false idols than worship the One Living and True God.

The writer of Hebrews associates the ascension of the Son of Man coming into the glory clouds of heaven, immediately worshipped by the angels, designated, "all you gods." Psalm 97 is prophetic in this way, directing the angels, gods, as Scripture uses, to show their inferiority to the Christ, the Son of God. Though Christ is made a little lower than the angels in human flesh, he is God incarnate and has been exalted in his work, approved in his resurrection, ascension and present standing at the right hand of the Ancient of Days as the Son of Man. Angels *should* worship him. In the psalm quoted, and in Hebrews 1:6, it is clear that both refer to divine worship. The angels are commanded to yield to Christ. The reason? It is utterly undeniable in the Covenant of Redemption that the Triune God set down before the world began that this eternal Son, given the Spirit without measure, in this exalted and ascended incarnated state is infinitely more excellent than any other being in creation, including the holy excellency of the angelic host. It is in fact God in the flesh. They, then, are to worship him. Worship him, all you gods, all you who are superior to men, demonstrate your commitment to the Father, the Son and the Spirit by giving homage to God's sole Anointed One introduced to the world – God in the flesh.

They had already seen the Son sitting high and lofty on the throne of Isaiah's prophetic vision and commission speaking of the Christ, the one who is holy, holy, holy (Isa. 6:1ff). Now, as might be said, in real time, upon his ascension into heaven as the exalted Son of Man riding on God's glory clouds, they are to bow and worship him for who he is. "I was watching in the night visions, and behold, One like the Son of Man, Coming with the clouds of heaven! He came to the Ancient of Days, and they brought Him near before Him," (Dan.

7:13).[1] The host of heaven ushered the Christ in worship up to the Ancient of Days. He is attended even by gate keepers, so to speak in Acts 1:10, "And while they looked steadfastly toward heaven as He went up, behold, two men stood by them in white apparel," (Acts 1:10). These are angels. From procession to his envelopment in heaven, the angels attended him; they worshipped him. There is this procession into the throne room of the Ancient of Days while the book of Hebrews instructs that such worship to this living Christ, this ascended God, must have his worship even by the angels for who he is. It is not left up to them to worship him or not. It is prophetically commanded. It is done to Christ by way of angelic duty. Because Christ is God, and the angels are inferior to God, they owe sacrifice and praise to him merely out of his exalted and holy eternal nature. "Let all the angels of God worship him." Angels are inferior; Christ is infinitely superior. The one worshipped is greater than the one worshipping. Angels worship him. Christ is greater than angels. The most excellent creatures must worship God in this special exalted state clothed in human flesh and riding the glory clouds.

When Christ was first declared to the world in his incarnation, God commanded even the most glorious angels to worship him. They did so because he is God. "And suddenly there was with the angel a multitude of the heavenly host praising God and saying: "Glory to

---

[1] For a fuller exposition of the Son of Man, see my work, "Seeing Christ Clearly."

God in the highest, And on earth peace, goodwill toward men on whom his favor rests!'" (Luke 2:13-14). Then, again, when he is resurrected, even firstborn from among the dead, the only begotten Son in the world manifested, "Let all the angels of God worship him." (Heb. 1:6). Divine angelic worship is due to Christ for who He is. Christ is the Son of God, true God; and the Father wills that all should honor the Son, even as they should honor the Father, (John 5:23). This includes the angels. What, then, does this have to do with human beings?

The doctrine we should consider here is that natural worship is given to Jesus Christ by the angels. Natural or divine worship is inseparably attached to the deity and being of God. He is the supreme excellency, the chief good, the first and best of beings. The angels know this and worship him incessantly for it. He is the Creator and Preserver of the angelic host, of the angels preserved by God in eternal happiness. It is the necessary character and nature of the angelic host to honor and worship that which is superior to them. They worship Christ, he who is superior, for his superiority, the first and best of beings. These preserved angels upheld from falling with the devil and his minions, always honor and obey the Lord Jesus. They did this throughout the Scriptures.

Francis Cheynell said, "It was the joy of the angels of heaven to be subject and serviceable unto Jesus

Christ."[2] When did they do this? Before the incarnation, an angel instructed Daniel was concerned with the Messiah, and how long it would be before his coming. (Dan. 9:24-25.) This angel served the Messiah in this way. As Paul instructs, when the fulness of time was come, an angel visits Mary, and said, "Fear not, Mary: for thou hast found favour with God. And, behold, thou shalt conceive in thy womb, and bring forth a son, and shalt call his name Jesus," (Luke 1:30-31). Upon the Christ's birth, the angelic host bring the glad tidings of the incarnation, and celebrate the incarnation, "Glory to God in the highest, and on earth peace, good-will toward men on whom his favor rests," (Luke 2:13-14).

When Christ was in danger of being killed by Herod, an angel warns Mary of the danger, and directs her to flee with Jesus into Egypt, (Matt. 2:13). The safety of the Anointed One was a great concern to the angelic host. Upon entrance into his earthly ministry, he was tempted by Satan forty days in the wilderness, and after that great battle vanquishing the evil one, "behold, angels came and ministered unto him," (Matt. 4:11). They gave a great ministry to the Anointed of God in humble service.

When he was hours before his crucifixion, in his agony in the garden, ready to take the cup of the wrath of the Father, "there appeared an angel from heaven

---

[2] Cheynell, Francis, *The Divine Triunity of the Father, Son and Holy Spirit*, (London: T.R., 1650) 54.

strengthening him," (Luke 22:43). He was ministered to by an angel just prior to the cross.

When Christ was dead, afterwards buried in the tomb, and the women came to the tomb the next day, as much as the angels announced his birth, so they announced his resurrection. "He is not here: for he is risen," (Matt. 28:6). They were eyewitnesses, in some capacity, to the celestial mysteries of the death of Christ and his glorious resurrection.

As noted before, the angels attended Christ's ascension into heaven, for they told the disciples, that as they saw him ascending into heaven, so he should come again from heaven in like manner, (Acts 1:11.).

And, in the text at hand in Hebrews 1:6, when Jesus ascends into the throne room of God for the first time as the exalted Christ, ushered in to judge, and take his place at the right hand of the power of God, to share in all eternal and infinite divine glory and power, there is an angelic procession where "all the angels worship him," (Heb. 1:6).

Now think, if angels serve and worship the Christ merely for who he is, and this is proven rather simply from the biblical texts, how much more shall *redeemed sinners* worship Christ for who he is and what he has done for them? This is something the angels *cannot* do, for angels have never been redeemed.

The second doctrine to consider here is that redeemed sinners are obliged to render to Christ natural and instituted worship for who he is and what he has done. If angels praise Christ incessantly for who he is as the eternal Son, now the exalted Son incarnate, God in the flesh, how much more should redeemed sinners worship him for not only who he is but what he has done for them personally? Angels are not redeemed. They have no capacity to worship based on redemption. They have no point of reference for being redeemed by the Lamb Slain before the foundation of the world. Angels are not converted, justified, sanctified, or glorified. Certainly, they long to look into these mysterious things, but redeemed sinners are directed to worship both naturally (Christ as God) by way of institution (because of his death and resurrection for them God prescribing particular worship to follow). God alone determines the manner in which sinners may approach him. Angels cannot worship in this way.

Consider that Christ will not share His glory with another. The angels worship Christ in all his glory. Isaiah 42:8 asserts, "I am the LORD: that is my name: and my glory will I not give to another, neither my praise to graven images." Worshipping the only true God, and none other, is accepted by Jesus, and he receives worship because he is God. It is his glory.

The Anointed Savior is worshipped all through Scripture. This is a remarkable fact for two reasons: Jesus elicited and allowed himself to be worshipped, which means he was God and knew this, and, only God is to be worshipped as the hundreds of Scriptural passages on the biblical subject prove. He is the expressed image of God and shares in the glory of the Lord. The fullness of God's glory shines from his very face as he reflects the being of God. God shares his glory with the Christ, because Christ is God. If Jesus was not God, then on this one point alone the entire Christian faith falls and turns to rubble. He is not merely a good teacher, or one with sound advice; by his own admission he is the GREAT I AM even before father Abraham was born. Jesus tells the disciples that they should believe in God as their object of faith, and believe in Him. In John 14:1 Jesus says, "Let not your heart be troubled: ye believe in God, believe also in me."

Belief in God is an act of worship and trust in his name. Jesus says that sinners should believe in him as they believe in God; they are one and the same. The element of faith is the same, and belief in Christ as God as Redeemer and Savior is all one. He is to be worshipped for such a truth. The angels cannot do this. In this trust, Jesus is magnified.

The Old Testament prophecy concerning the Son in Psalm 2:12 is helpful in this, "Kiss the Son, lest he be angry, and ye perish from the way, when his wrath is kindled but a little. Blessed are all they that put their trust in him." Those who trust the Son are called blessed. He is to be kissed, or *praised.* The Son is to be worshipped and trusted because he is God; both for who he is and what he has done for redeemed sinners. Christ is to be honored in the same way as the Father, as John 5:22 demonstrates, "That all men should honour the Son, even as they honour the Father. He that honoureth not the Son honoureth not the Father which hath sent him." The Triune Godhead, Father, Son and Spirit are to be equally honored, and this could not be done unless Christ is God. Otherwise men would give the honor to a mere man that which would be due to God alone. Such is *blasphemy*. It was the very thing the Jews thought, when Christ said he was God, the great I AM, and they desired to kill him because "he made himself equal with God;" they *understood* what he was saying. The angels keenly understand who Jesus is in their obligation to worship Christ as God. They are commanded to worship him naturally as God. In fact, all creatures are commanded to bow down to him and worship him naturally, "all shall bow to Him wherefore God also hath highly exalted him, and given him a name which is above every name: That at the name of Jesus every knee should bow, of things in heaven, and things in earth, and things under the earth; And that every tongue should confess that Jesus Christ is Lord, to the glory of God the Father," (Philippians 2:9–11). Christ as Lord shall be worshipped by all. All knees will be forced to bow, or they will bow willingly, to the Lord.

This is also seen in Revelation 5:13, "And every creature which is in heaven, and on the earth, and under the earth, and such as are in the sea, and all that are in them, heard I saying, Blessing, and honour, and glory, and power, be unto him that sitteth upon the throne, and unto the Lamb forever and ever." The Lamb, Christ, is worshipped forever and ever because He is God, naturally.

When he walked the earth, the Anointed Savior was worshipped often. A leper worshipped him in Matthew 8:2, "And, behold, there came a leper and worshipped him, saying, Lord, if thou wilt, thou canst make me clean." A ruler worshipped him in Matthew 9:18, "While he spake these things unto them, behold, there came a certain ruler, and worshipped him, saying, my daughter is even now dead: but come and lay thy hand upon her, and she shall live." The disciples worshipped him in Matthew 14:33, "Then they that were in the ship came and worshipped him, saying, of a truth thou art the Son of God." A Canaanite woman worshipped him in Matthew 15:25, "Then came she and worshipped him, saying, Lord, help me." Demons even worshipped him as with the Gadarene Demoniac, "But when he saw Jesus afar off, he ran and worshipped him," (Mark 5:6). A poor blind man who was healed, worshipped him, "And he said, Lord, I believe. And he worshipped him," (John 9:38). In Matthew 28:9, 17, after the resurrection, the disciples worshipped him again, "And as they went to tell his disciples, behold, Jesus met them, saying, All hail. And they came and held him by the feet, and worshipped him. And when they saw him, they worshipped him: but some doubted." The idea that some doubted is utterly amazing! On the road to Emmaus the two disciples worshipped him in Luke

24:52, "And they worshipped him, and returned to Jerusalem with great joy."

Jesus allowed and expected men to worship him, and elicited that worship. This is something an Israelite would have been stoned for, and the Jews certainly desired to stone Jesus as a result of his words and their hardness of heart. Demons, angels, lepers, Gentiles, Jews, his own disciples, and so on, worshiped him. Over and over we see that Jesus Christ was worshipped, and those who worshipped him acted accordingly – he deserved to be worshipped because he is naturally God.

What about redeemed sinners who know that he is God and yet they are also instructed by him through Scripture to worship as he so institutes it as a result of his redemptive work? Yes, Jesus is naturally worshipped by the angels as God; and by others. But, redeemed sinners are also instructed to worship him in a particular manner for God's glory because of the work of redemption. Only redeemed sinners can do this, and they must do it as God prescribes to exalt the Anointed Savior. He must be glorified in worship in a particular manner by redeemed sinners in God's instituted worship. Christ must have his worship, both kinds; natural and instituted. God calls his angels to do it, but they are limited to the first way, God naturally. But redeemed sinners must do it more. The angel's natural worship is grounded on the knowledge of Christ's glorious nature. Instituted worship is grounded on the revelation of the will of God to people who have been saved from sin and death and hell. Christ is to be worshipped by redeemed sinners very particularly as God institutes in his church in a special way as prescribed by his word. The angels cannot do this.

When God has manifested his will in the way he will be worshipped as the exalted Christ, that way of worship is instituted worship; and redeemed sinners must outdo the angels in that they worship Christ naturally as God, and, instituted by God for being the Anointed Messiah and their Savior. Redeemed Sinners must honor the Son in God's instituted worship because of his work and his atonement. The redeemed sinner who will honor Christ must make it his business to know Christ and his work. They are to study the knowledge of God in order to have high thoughts of Christ's work and merit for them. They are to know his infinite excellence in both his nature and his work. The highest way a redeemed sinner can worship Christ is to make sure that they think God's thoughts about Christ after him, having high thoughts of God on both accounts; because of who he is and what he has done. The angels cannot do this.

Worship is not merely an outward action in bowing the head, praying, singing the psalm, hearing the word, taking the supper and such. All this is *heart work*. It comes from a renewed nature that only a redeemed sinner possesses. They were lost, going to hell, and then God saved them, and is carrying them to heaven through

Christ. They have new hearts as a result of this, born from above, and regenerated by the power of God.

This inward worship of God from the heart for who he is and what he has done, in high thoughts and contemplations of his majesty, is the manner in which the highest way of worship is expressed. "And we know that the Son of God has come and has given us an understanding, that we may know Him who is true; and we are in Him who is true, in His Son Jesus Christ. This is the true God and eternal life," (1 John 5:20). The angels cannot do this.

The redeemed sinner intimately knows Christ, and believes solely on Christ for his salvation. It is Christ alone (sola Christus), through the merit of his work (sola gratia), God incarnate in the flesh, who must be believed and worshipped. He exhorts, "You believe in God, believe also in me," (John 14:1). In the depravity of their lost state, sinners who have had a heart transformation (a spiritual surgery) and are seeking the fullness of redemption, look and believe on Christ alone. They do not need to wage a war, or work a work, or pay a price, or add anything to the exalted Messiah's work. As the Anointed Savior says, "This is the work of God, that you believe in Him whom He sent," (John 6:29). This is to honor the Son as to honor the Father.

Christ, through faith, through belief, plunders the kingdom of darkness, and renders the sinner capable of believing on the most sublime doctrine in all the bible – the covenant work of the exalted Anointed Savior. The

Father seeks worshippers to worship his Christ in spirit and truth for who he is and what he has done. This is to worship without the shadows of the temple, and in the truth of God's instituted worship. Many times, sinners come to faith first believing what Christ did as God, but then later realize the infinite excellencies of Christ as God. This is fine, and life is about learning more about Christ. Yet, consider, true faith on Christ is powered by the Holy Spirit, and he, as a refiner and purifier, purges away all those old corruptions, killing the old man of sin, and making the sinner a new creation in the Beloved. The redeemed sinner in this loves the Lord Jesus Christ in sincerity for his merit, imputation of alien righteousness to them, and expiation of sin, and they worship him for it. The angels cannot do this.

The redeemed sinner loves Jesus in sincerity by grace. "Grace be with all those who love our Lord Jesus Christ in sincerity. Amen," (Eph. 6:24). Isaiah says, "Now will I sing unto my well-beloved," (Isa. 5:1). Who is this? It is the Lord Jesus Christ. Worship due to Christ is an exercise in acts of sincere love through grace; he is the well-beloved; redeemed sinners *love* him. Such a love loves Christ in all situations and is cultivated by the power of the Spirit of grace. Loving him in times of plenty. Loving him in times of want. Loving him in times of affliction. Loving him in times of blessing. One preacher said, "Jesus Christ is not always honey; he is sometimes bitter myrrh." Yet, this Jesus is worshipped by redeemed sinners for it all. Difficult, or easy, they worship Christ for what he has done in redeeming them, and, pressing them into his image. The angels cannot do this.

The redeemed sinner must ascribe all glory to him and give him thanks which is set inside God's instituted worship of the Christ due to his work. "Worthy is the Lamb that was slain to receive power, and riches, and wisdom, and strength, and honor, and glory, and blessing," (Rev. 5:12-13). Redeemed sinners in such a cry of worship due to his redemption are blessed and are in the most happy condition of eternal life. They have very high thoughts of him; they know through the blood of the cross, and the resurrection from the dead, from his ascension into heaven, and present intercession for them, that they have been translated from the dominion of darkness into the kingdom of the beloved. And they love him for this. They worship him in the most holy manner they are able through the Spirit in the prescription of the Father's will. Because they know that such worship will bring the most glory to the Anointed Savior. The angels cannot do this.

The redeemed sinner acknowledges that Christ alone has been appointed by God to build his church. Redeemed sinners are part of his church. They are part of his mystical covenanted body. Much of the honor that redeemed sinners give the Christ is because he is the builder of his church, and so many blessings are annexed to it. "The man whose name is the Branch, he shall build the temple of the Lord," (Zech. 6:12). Christ is exalted as the builder of his church and its supplier and its caretaker and its keeper. He is exalted and worshipped by Redeemed sinners for his church work. The angels cannot do this.

Redeemed sinners partake of the sacraments and ordinances of Christ in his church in divine worship. Christ alone, as the exalted Messiah has the power to set down and command redeemed sinners to worship in a particular manner. Christ sets such ordinances up or tears them down. He tears down the temple, and sets up the supper. He fulfills the sacrament of circumcision as "the type" and instead sets down the ordinance of baptism. It is not up to men to institute anything in his church. It is Christ's redeemed bride, and no man may play the harlot with his worship. When men do this, they dishonor Christ and deny him the honor of God's prescribed and instituted worship. In doing such, and offering false worship to Christ, they worship him in vain, Jesus says in Matthew 15. They set up as he calls it, "an image of jealousy," (Ezek. 8:3). All human inventions placed in God's instituted worship to Christ are images of jealousy which God hates; he does not tolerate it. God's hatred is a subsequent working of the absence of love. God would much rather see redeemed sinners worship according to his prescription. He loves that. Such worship brings God great glory.

The vain mind does injury to Christ in instituting such deviant and un-glorifying aspects to worship. It changes it. It makes worship more palatable to personal taste. It makes it more attractive and worldly. God hates that because he has no love for it. Men cannot set worship up or rescind any aspect of worship in Christ's church. Only Christ is able to do this and is glorified and worshipped as a result of it.

Consider the ordinance of the Lord's Supper. The supper is direct worship and communion due to Christ in remembrance of what he did in redeeming his people. What worship is due to him for this? It is a sacrament, a religious mystery, appointed only for those that believe on the Lord Jesus for salvation by grace through faith, in divine worship of the Anointed One. The angels cannot do this.

The doctrine of Scripture, taught by holy men, and the apostles of our Lord, demonstrate that natural worship and instituted worship are due only to God, only to Christ. Those that worship him, draw near to him, in any part of divine worship, and they must do so with high thoughts prescribed and set down by the will of the Lord, and with no others. Since Jesus Christ, the only Head of the church, is her glorious Lord, the Only Begotten Son of the living God; he ought to be worshipped by redeemed sinners as God instructs. In doing this, redeemed sinners are instructed to do things in worship that even the most glorious angels cannot do.

Natural worship and instituted worship are commanded by God. God requires you as a created being to worship Christ naturally. You worship him for who he is. The Bible has revealed God to us, and so instructs us as to his character, being and will. On this alone you are to worship him. On this alone your studies take you through his attributes, and this presses worship to him because he is the great I AM. Yet, as redeemed sinners, God requires you to worship Christ by his instituted means. He requires you to worship him in a particular manner. In Scripture, and subsequently in our Confession, these truths are laid out so that there is no question on what *Gospel Worship* entails. None. One either follows it or rejects it. The Father seeks worshippers to worship him. You he has sought out for worship and you have come to worship him in the way he has outlined in Scripture. God alone determines these things. There is no other way of acceptably worshipping God other than the way he has prescribed. You recognize this and embrace it. You should be dedicated to casting aside everything that would impinge on God's holy desire of worship to his Anointed. Is it not interesting that God does not "seek saved individuals?" God first seeks *worshippers* Christ says. Implied in this is that right worship is accomplished by those born again. John 3 comes before John 4. Calvin said, "If it is inquired, then, by what things chiefly the Christian religion has a standing existence among us, and maintains its truth, it will be found that the following two not only occupy the principal place, but comprehend under them all the other parts, and consequently the whole substance of Christianity, viz., a knowledge, first, of the mode in which God is duly worshipped; and, secondly, of the source from which salvation is to be obtained. I know how difficult it is to persuade the world that God disapproves of all modes of worship not expressly sanctioned by his word."[3] Worship is set down first, then salvation second. That order is highlighted based on what the Bible reveals about what God desires. It's all about God, and his Anointed Savior.

We know that proper worship prescribed by God is only attainable by Spirit-empowered Christians worshipping through the word. But biblically, even from Genesis 4 with Cain and Abel in the very first worship service, God is looking for what he says is acceptable worship. And if worship is acceptable to him, will not you be accepted if you do well in it? Such worship you may offer, even that which angels cannot do. But only if you hold to the truth.

If you worship in a church that upholds the integrity of the Scriptures, you worship in a church that is an anomaly to surrounding churches all over the country. God knows for this kind of believer, that you worship him not only for who he is naturally, but you do so and seek to do so by the manner in which he has instituted in his word. In this, your desires are uncompromising. You go to a church to worship in a manner that you cannot find in any church for a hundred

---

[3] Calvin, John, *The Necessity of Reforming the Church*, https://www.apuritansmind.com/puritan-worship/the-necessity-of-reforming-the-church-part-1-by-dr-john-calvin/.

miles in any direction. This places faithful Christians into such an adoring manner to the Savior who has brought together *faithful* worshippers. It is the sad state of the church and the disparagement that professing Christians have of God's instituted worship, that there are not more churches who worship in a manner higher than the angelic host.

Churches know that God is to be worshipped for who he is. They will acquiesce to what the angels did in bowing before the Christ. But, God alone determines the manner in which you, redeemed sinners, approach him. And that is quite particular. Calvin again said, "I know how difficult it is to persuade the world that God disapproves of all modes of worship not expressly sanctioned by his word."[4]

One brother was asked, "What do you normally find in stalwart Reformed Churches?" His answer was "few people." Because people would rather have a little worldly trash in their worship, rather than God's instituted prescription. You must be conformed to that prescription that God has laid down to worship his one and only Anointed Savior, and you must never deviate from it. The angels never deviate from the natural worship they give Christ. They were designed to worship the holy one as holy. You must never deviate from worshipping Christ in Spirit (not according to any shadows of the temple) and truth (according to his

---

[4] Ibid.

prescribed institution). All knees in heaven shall bow to Christ as they engage his holiness.

Here on earth, you are to bow voluntarily but particularly, as a body to worship him in a manner in which he requires, in a manner greater than the angels. This is one of the two main staples of the Christian religion recovered by the Reformation. Not that it was wholly destitute, as God always keeps his 7000 from bowing the knee to Baal. But in its widening influence it was sparked again by the Reformers who went back to Scripture to uphold true worship of the Christ.

Is this doctrine, then, useful to us? Redeemed sinners are obliged to render to Christ natural and instituted worship for who he is and what he has done. It is preeminently useful for us who worship the Anointed Savior as God so requires; it is *your life*. The Anointed Savior's doctrine is increasing with the faithful, while all idolatry and everything opposed to the faith of Christ is daily dwindling, and losing power, and falling into darkness. Christians ought to worship the Savior, "Who is above all" and "mighty," even God, the Living Word, condemning all those who are being vanquished and done away by him because of their idolatry.

Now, the divine appearing of the Word of God has come, and the darkness of the idolatry can never be allowed to prevail. Christ is God, the Word, the Power of God, the Redeemer, and blood-soaked Savior. He who is to be worshipped for who he is and what he has done by you. These things, are only useful if we do more than the angels do in God's prescription of instituted worship. There are myriads of churches that come together to worship in ways of idolatry with hearty intentions to serve God in the way they think is right, and God is not in the midst of it. God, in Ezekiel, rails against such churches that do this: "Therefore, as I live,' says the Lord GOD, 'surely, because you have defiled My sanctuary with all your detestable things and with all your abominations, therefore I will also diminish you; My eye will not spare, nor will I have any pity.'" (Ezek. 5:11). He has no pity, no spiritual power in any of the means of grace. Diminish in number, diminish in spiritual power? They diminish in God's visitation to them. "Furthermore He said to me, "Son of man, do you see what they are doing, the great abominations that the house of Israel commits here, to make Me go far away from My sanctuary?" (Ezek. 8:6). God *leaves* idolatrous services no matter what the intention of the people in that service is. He makes the means of grace of no affect in such places. He doesn't attend their idolatrous services. It greatly concerns us that we render him his due. "By those who come near Me I must be regarded as holy; And before all the people I must be glorified" (Lev. 10:3). It is our privilege to do so as redeemed sinners. "For who makes you to differ from another?" (1 Cor. 4:7).

The very worship you bring, higher than the angels, more than the angelic host, is a direct result of Christ Jesus making you to differ from others. Not everyone is saved. In God's sovereign choice he chose you to serve him in natural worship and instituted worship of His Son. How will you take up that mantle and glorify God? With what zeal, passion, desire, preparation, power? What will you do to God's Christ that angels cannot do? Will you out-praise them? Will you out do them?

God does at times remove or abandon false churches? Consider, it is Jesus Christ alone that can unchurch a church. It is he that threatens it, "I will remove your candlestick out of this place, except you repent," (Rev. 2:5). The seven candlesticks are the seven churches, so that to remove the candlestick is to take away the church. It is Christ alone that can "call them Loammi," (not my people) (Hos. 1:9). It belongs to Jesus Christ alone to give to a church a bill of divorce. And for any to undertake to pronounce Loammi where Christ has not done it, is to sin highly against Christ's church. We must be very careful in announcing "Ichabod" from places we think propagate unfit worship. We can theologically state what is unfit and demonstrate what is unfit, and make judgments about what God says is not fitting for his worship, for the majesty of Jesus Christ. But we are not God. We are not the judge of the earth. We may make judgments, but make them in a directed manner very carefully and with much wisdom. We bow before the sovereign God who still has his Corinthians and his Thyatiras. Instead, take it to heart yourselves. Think about the judgments against the church in

Scripture to be possibilities to you. They are warnings to you as a Christian in a church. If it were not for the grace of God and his word, where would you be? What would you be doing? Where would you be worshipping Christ even now? How might you guard yourselves against declension in worship? How might you guard against idolatry?

Consider that God requires that you honor the Son even as you honor the Father, seeing he is equal to him in the point of honor. And if you will do so, you must in this way honor him with natural and instituted worship. You may not take license in this as so many do. You must be on guard against every possibility of change or deviation in it. Every change negates it as worship. Every change to God's prescription ushers in idolatry. I think that not many people, not many professing Christians take this to heart. They tend to settle for what they have wherever they are. This is a tragedy since God is seeking true *worshippers*. Even if they know it, they are content to stay in a place, in a church, that is outwardly deviant because it's the best thing in the area they have. God is looking for worshippers, and yet, what are *they* doing in neglecting that?

I'd encourage everyone in such a situation to take to heart the warnings of the Lord, and instead make the move to a church and fellowship for the expansion of the kingdom in a holy manner; and that might mean making a move to another place, or state, or country, to worship with those who honor the Lord. Never settle. God does not settle. Those who settle give up their ability to do more than the angels. God never promises to keep a church in a specific location. God never promises that those who commit idolatry, that he is in their midst regardless of their intentions. In all actuality he promises quite the opposite. To the churches in Revelation he tells them to *repent.* To the church in the Temple in Ezekiel he tells them to *repent.* To his very church and people he says that those who are joined to idolatry he leaves them alone (Hosea 4:17), not even to bother with them. But for you, I suspect much greater things than all of that. In a certain way, in a humble way, in a wise way, when God says "Let all the angels of God worship Him," so you say, "I will do so and much more."

Say: I will do it faithfully. I will do it with great devotion. I will do it with great fervor. I will do it passionately. I will do it constantly. Incessantly, persistently, perpetually. I will do it both now and forever. I will worship this Christ greater than the angels, for I will worship him because of who he is, AND how he has particularly instructed me in the high thoughts of worship to the Redeemer and Savior for what he has done by his divine prescription.

This is why God has given his people places that are faithful in their worship. He loves you, has blessed you abundantly, and desires to see the fruit of righteousness working out in adoration of his Son in this place. That the very walls of the church themselves would soak up your fastidious prayers, your singing of psalms, the word taught and preached, the sacraments used faithfully, the work of God glorified, and the like. Prove out, then, your devotion to him and his Christ as he so desires, for the angels cannot do this, but you can.

Mark 4: Gospel Worship Part 2

"O sing unto the LORD a new song: sing unto the LORD, all the earth," (Psa. 96:1).

In the last chapter, I gave you some basic concepts about worship, and how that worship should "out worship" the angels. In this chapter, I'd like to cover a continuation of that idea in a practical manner. We begin with Psalm 96. The testimony of Psalm 96 is quite rich. This Psalm gathers up into a summary a response by the Christian of who God is and what God has done. It furnishes his people with *a theology of praise.* Do you have a theology of praise?

Psalm 96 is a song, a psalm, a hymn; all those mean the very same thing. The roots of its message rests in 1 Chronicles 16 where David brought the ark into the tabernacle. He praised God for his presence and composed this psalm, of which he used part of this psalm in the dedication of the ark, as well as parts of Psalms 105, and 106. It was a spiritual song of thanksgiving for his great victory over the Philistines and a resting place for the ark of God. This often symbolized God's presence with his people. The psalm in 1 Chronicles 16 is considerably longer than the psalm here in 96. It runs on from 1 Chronicles 16:8 all the way to verse 36. Psalm 96 is only part of it from the 23rd to the 33rd verse. Some think this Psalm was used during the dedication of the second temple since the psalm in the Septuagint, Vulgate, Æthiopic and Arabic versions has a superscription on it, "A song of David when the house was built after the captivity."

This psalm is interchangeably designated as a spiritual song to worship God. Israel is encouraged to give praise and thanks to the Lord. This is to call on his name, and to make known (publicly) among the peoples his deeds (v. 8). This is done in singing to him, sing praise to him, and talk of all his wonderful works (v. 9). This is done to glory in his holy name, to let those who seek rejoice (v. 10). These people look to the Lord and his strength, seek his face continually (v. 11), remember the marvelous works he has done, his miracles, and the judgments of his mouth (v. 12). We have the author directing God's people to sing to the Lord a new song in the summary version of Psalm 96. David is declared as the author and the time of his composition was given as the occasion – the time when he appointed Asaph and his brethren for musical responsibilities in the tabernacle (*cf.* 1 Chronicles 16:7). "On that day David first delivered this psalm into the hand of Asaph and his brethren, to thank the LORD," (1 Chron. 16:7).

Strictly speaking, this is not a new song today. For example, "Also in the day of the firstfruits, when ye bring a new meat offering unto the LORD, after your weeks be out, ye shall have an holy convocation; ye shall do no servile work." The offering brought was new, but bringing offerings is not a new thing (Numbers 28:26). It holds the connotation as something being renewed, or better yet, refreshed. Old things done or seen in a new light or new perspective. Take for example Lamentations 3:22-23, "It is of the LORD'S mercies that we are not consumed, because his compassions fail not. They are new every morning: great is thy faithfulness." The Lord *renews* mercy? His mercy gets old so he has to make new mercy to replace old mercy? It's new every morning isn't it? Not in *that* way. Is his mercy really new or is it the continued view of his salvation seen in light of the "new" day or "new help" from the perspective of the one considering it? There are new moons (Ezek. 45:17), new kings (Exod. 1:8), and new songs. But these songs are not new in substance. Newness can be seen in a variety of ways, all of which are true, but they hold a connotation of something that exists which is considered in a fresh way.

This Psalm instructs the church to sing what may be called new because it is adapted for this new purpose, and new mercies are given to the people of God in worship. As with Rev. 5:9-10, "And they sang a new song, saying: "You are worthy to take the scroll, And to open its seals; For You were slain, And have redeemed us to God by Your blood Out of every tribe and tongue and people and nation, And have made us kings and priests to our God; And we shall reign on the earth."" This theological idea is *not* new. It is the atonement of the Messiah that has saved people out of every tribe tongue and nation, people from all the earth, and yet, they sing a new song? Is this redeeming power of God not seen part and parcel of Psalm 96? How it is *new?*

It is equally important that it is a psalm which points forward to the fulfillment of Jesus Christ in the Gospel. It causes the reader to consider the new covenant era coming, the completion of the fulfillment of the eternal covenant in the Anointed One, the Savior. Eternal covenant, new covenant? Is it *new?* If it is eternal, is it new? Or is it by perspective? It is not simply directed to the Jews, nor for the time only of the Jews at the temple, but, in light of all nations. In this way it has a direct, now and not yet, fulfillment with its reference to the kingdom of Christ.

This renewed view of the worship of God in light of the Christ who is coming, at the time for the Psalmist, is for the church the One who came and fulfills this worship where all the earth praises him collectively. In this light, old truths seem so new. What would Paul be thinking after his conversion of the Old Testament that he had read so often with *new eyes?* In this psalm it speaks, not of just Israel, but all the earth. This is certainly a new perspective. It is a fulfilled perspective. There are literally hundreds of instances in the Psalms alone where we find praise directed toward God for who he is and what he has done in the eternal covenant, now in the hands of the new testator, Jesus, for all the earth; prophetic passages with a new meaning to praise God.

Praise is a common designation of worship. Psalm 7:17 says, "I will praise the LORD according to his righteousness: and will sing praise to the name of the LORD most high." Psalm 9:2 says, "I will be glad and rejoice in thee: I will sing praise to thy name, O thou most High." Psalm 21:13 exclaims, "Be thou exalted, LORD, in thine own strength: so will we sing and praise thy power." Those who come together to praise God are doing so, as the psalm instructs, as those from all over the earth. The church is to praise him encompassing the entire terrestrial ball, the whole earth. Psalm 22:22 (*cf.* Psalm 35:18), "I will declare thy name unto my brethren: in the midst of the congregation will I praise thee," and, Psalm 22:25, "My praise shall be of thee in the great congregation." The great congregation is not only the church, but the mass of the visible manifestation of the church on the earth. The church is instructed to praise God together. It is true, that independently people may praise God, they may sing of him in their home, or in their car, but God is more interested in hearing praise from the whole earth. It is a collective refrain in the psalm.

Such praise is accomplished, as the Psalter instructs, indiscriminately before all kinds of people, Psalm 57:9, "I will praise thee, O Lord, among the people: I will sing unto thee among the nations." Such praise by the church is because of who he is and what he has done, Psalm 66:2, "Sing forth the honour of his name: make his praise glorious." The entire earth is to involve themselves in singing praise to God, Psalm 107:8, "Oh that men would praise the LORD for his goodness, and for his wonderful works to the children of men!" and, Psalm 117:1, "O praise the LORD, all ye nations: praise him, all ye people." Psalm 47:7, "For God is the King of all the earth: sing ye praises with understanding." The book of Hebrews sums up this public praise conveniently when it says, "By him *[that is Christ]* therefore let us offer the sacrifice of praise to God continually, that is, the fruit of our lips giving thanks to his name," (Heb. 13:15). The Greek word for praise here (αἰνέσεως) means *a thank offering.*

Formally speaking, praise is a collective response to God by the church. Praise is a form of expression for what the Psalmist knows about God according to truth. Individuals can certainly do this, but it is set in the context of the church and the assembly. Yet, it says, "all the earth." Hold that thought for a moment.

If one knows little about God, they shall worship little in praise to him no matter how long they may sing or how many songs they sing. Scripture instructs that the earth, the church, knows Him by His word. "And we know that the Son of God is come, and hath given us an understanding, that we may know him that is true, and we are in him that is true, even in his Son Jesus Christ. This is the true God, and eternal life," (1 John 5:20). Thomas Ford, one of the Westminster Divines, said in his work, *The Singing of Psalms the Duty of Christians,*

"None can sing a Psalm as he ought, unless he has grace in his heart, and is renewed in the spirit of his mind."[1]

Both must be present in order to sing praise to God in the manner God has required. In God's prescription for worship, he seeks a collective worship experience by a collective body of *praisers*. No longer do church goers *look on* to see other people sing as they did in the temple. No, the temple is over. Now, they sing, the whole world sings, or should, to give praise to God. There is no praise by substitution in this way. There are no stand-ins. Priests no longer "do things" for onlookers. They all are to sing out.

It is interesting that Psalm 96 says this about Gospel truths; all the earth in the time of the good news of the Anointed Savior shall sing in this way. It is interesting that the priests would have sung this at the temple while onlookers looked and listened. In doing this, worship by Scripture song helps the church to know God more and express praise both intellectually, and emotionally. They are required to sing his word and sing about high thoughts of God. They sing God's thoughts after him. This is what God looks for in his church. How might God be magnified and reflected in the song of his people. Even in verse 2 of this psalm, it says, "Sing to the LORD, bless His name; Proclaim the good news of His salvation from day to day," (Psa. 96:2).

---

[1] Ford, Thomas, *The Singing of Psalms the Duty of Christians*, (Coconut Creek, FL: Puritan Publications, 2012) 56.

When one learns something new of God's name, this same song becomes new to the one singing.

Consider, this use of praise to God is accomplished and instructed to the "all the earth." As Scripture interprets Scripture, we know that all men are not regenerate. They are born as enemies of God, under the Covenant of Works in Adam, and have God's wrath abiding on them until they are saved and changed by God's Spirit of Grace. Only regenerate people are able to fulfill this directive (any biblical directive in the Psalm to sing a new song, or as verses 2-3 says, they bless, proclaim and declare wonders about God). They bless God. They proclaim the good news of God's Messiah. They declare his glory among the nations.

Such a psalm, then, demonstrates the manner in which the kingdom of Christ, collectively on the earth, testifies through their worship about the being of the creator, and the redemptive wonders of his Anointed Savior.

In contrast to this collective group which is brought together for praise from "all the earth" is the carnal mind that is at enmity with God. These are, "those ... in the flesh [who] cannot please God," (Rom. 8:8). They do not have the ability to fulfill this declaration, proclamation, or blessing as part of the corporate body of worshippers. Only born again individuals can do this. Proclaiming and declaring God's being and his redemptive work is a primary aspect of *praise*. It reflects back to God what he wants to see in his people, and if those people do not have it, God calls such, *a sacrifice of wickedness*. Yet, those not converted have no excuse *not* to praise God. They are simply in rebellion against him and do not want to. God is *owed* natural worship from such people.

Praise is not only to proclaim and declare, but it is the proper tool to bless God. Although an individual church sings such praise to magnify God in their public worship on the Lord's Day, and it may tend to be sufficient to edify itself for a time, God does not see this as solely sufficient in light of his glory. It is not sufficient to glorify God alone in this way. Instead, he requires and desires that the church, collectively, from all the earth, praise him jointly, or at least have an eye to this as the psalm so prophecies about the Gospel era. This is a holding onto the "not yet" of the Gospel age. It is looking forward to the fulfillment of joining together with every tribe tongue and nation to bless God for all time.

In this way, biblical Worship, as a body is the due response of rational creatures to the self-revelation of their Creator. How many bodies does Christ have? one; yet on the earth that body is geographically divided up. Here on earth the church tenders up praise and reverence to him which is his due. This is done, according to God's desire, among all the earth; from people all over the globe in corporate worship as they follow his instituted worship. That is the consequence of being on this earth, at this time, and must be done in local bodies. They are unable to render to God praise in a manner corporately as one single body physically. They are still scattered right now.

This idea of singing to the Lord in this way, to bless, proclaim and declare, is repeated in the psalm. This shows God's mind in preferring such public worship across the earth to all other kinds of worship. It is in triplicate, like Isaiah 6 and the cry of the seraphim, "holy, holy, holy." Whenever Scripture wishes to catch the reader's attention to God's desire, or an important statement, it repeats itself. "Truly, Truly I say unto you..." as Jesus often did. In this psalm, it is like placing a triple exclamation point at the end of a sentence in English. In Hebrew there is repetition, and repetition becomes exclamation. The focus is given to the Lord in whom the church praises. They sing to the Lord. Everyone across the lands are to sing to him together. How do they do this if they are not currently in heaven in the consummation of all ages, or able to have a unified worship service across the face of the planet? They do this in the local body. "Let us go into His tabernacle; Let us worship at His footstool," (Psa. 132:7). "Come, and let us go up to the mountain of the LORD," (Isa. 2:3). They come in smaller groups, to praise God corporately now.

What is the substance of their singing? God as God. God is the great I AM. He is the first and best of beings. He is most glorious. God has revealed his salvation to the earth and the earth is required to give God praise for this. God has revealed his salvation to the church and the collective church across the earth is required to give God praise. Keep in mind, in the time of David's writing, the nations around Israel were not part of God's theocracy, or his instituted means of grace, which at the time was at the temple. They were left in darkness. But in these Gospel times, Gentiles have been brought in, as those among, "all people" to sing praises to God, and to Christ. In such a response of praise David could not quote this Psalm in all its fullness when he was praising God in 1 Chronicles 16, for it was a celebration for Israel at the time. Yet David knew, and even composed this, in prophecy knowing that it is also a song for the Gentiles in the age of the Messiah, where it is for all the earth; an old psalm *in a new way.* All the regenerate sing; Jew or Gentile, male or female, slave or free, *etc.* Revelation 7:9 says, "After these things I looked and behold, a great multitude which no one could number, from all nations, tribes, peoples, and tongues standing before the lamb...and crying out..." They were crying out, giving great praise. This is the glorious outcome of the spread of the Gospel because of the work of Jesus, God's Anointed Savior.

It is a glorious outcome of this prophetic psalm that Gentiles will sing such psalms, hymns, songs in praise to God. Not only Jews who are happy to have the presence of the ark back in Jerusalem, but all kinds of people. "Go ye therefore, and teach all nations, baptizing them in the name of the Father, and of the Son, and of the Holy Ghost: Teaching them to observe all things whatsoever I have commanded you," (Matthew 28:19-

20). That means the church must, 1) know what Christ has taught his church (and that's a tall order since it is contained in the 66 books of the Bible), and 2) that they testify to the nations what Christ has commanded them about himself. In this, the church has a monumental responsibility that is eternally relevant. Their responsibility not only centers around knowledge and praise, but takes up the witness to the truth that the Father seeks more worshippers. As Jesus said, "But the hour cometh, and now is, when the true worshippers shall worship the Father in spirit and in truth: for the Father seeketh such to worship him," (John 4:23).

What, is a faithful doctrine to pull from this particular text? Consider that corporate worship is a picture of the eternal nature of praise to God through Christ's redemptive covenant.

The church should have a high view of corporate worship over any other kind. They are required to be imitators of God as beloved children, in this way, they are to mimic God's view of worship. God's view of worship on the earth surrounds his refracted glory. People are to glimmer a little, metaphorically, in singing out about him; they are to reflect him in praise.

How will redeemed sinners praise God and give his name glory? God has a very high view of corporate worship over any other kind. I will give you some reasons for this:

[1] He places a high esteem on seeking worshippers for corporate worship. The place where

God's name dwells no longer serves as a type or sign of the coming Messiah. The Messiah has come. Anything in which God's name was attached in the Old Testament, which was a type or sign of Christ to come, is now abolished. There is no more need for temples, sacrifices, *etc.* This is why Christ told the Samaritan woman that, "the hour is coming, and now is, when the true worshipers will worship the Father in spirit and truth; for the Father is seeking such to worship Him," (John 4:23-24). Worship is done by truth and through the Spirit. This is the kind of worship the Father seeks. And it is accomplished in the corporate assembly of Christ's mystical body; both now, and not yet. Now, it is in geographic locations, and not yet, it will be in heaven.

Consider this psalm which is very important in connection with this public praise. "The LORD loves the gates of Zion more than all the dwellings of Jacob," (Psa. 87:2). The entrance to the corporate setting of worship is more esteemed by God than private devotions. He is more interested in such glory from his corporate body; the bride of Christ. But even now, he does not have it as collectively as it will be in heaven. Now he has some, but they are not all voiced together. God highly esteems corporate worship as that which glorifies him most, now, by his people. Yet the Christian must have an eye to the not yet where it will be done to God in perfection, wholly and completely as the single mystical body joined in eternity to sing praise to Christ forever later on.

[2] God will have his glory, and he will have it to its fullest stature. God is most glorified by his collective people across the face of the earth. God is certainly glorified by individuals, but he is much more glorified by his collective church. "Gather My saints together to Me, Those who have made a covenant with Me by sacrifice...Call upon Me in the day of trouble; I will deliver you, and you shall glorify Me,'" (Psa. 50:5, 15). God seeks the most glory. "All nations whom You have made Shall come and worship before You, O Lord, and shall glorify Your name," (Psa. 86:9). The collective church is to glorify God's name, and this argues the conversion of the Gentiles which happens at the time of the coming of Christ. "Who shall not fear You, O Lord, and glorify Your name? For You alone are holy. For all nations shall come and worship before You, For Your judgments have been manifested," (Rev. 15:4). God, rightly seeks that which is best. What is best? That is his glory above all things. "I am the LORD, that is My name; and My glory I will not give to another, Nor My praise to carved images," (Isa. 42:8).

Consider Paul's exhortation, "Now I say that Jesus Christ has become a servant to the circumcision for the truth of God, to confirm the promises made to the fathers, and that the Gentiles might glorify God for His mercy, as it is written: "For this reason I will confess to You among the Gentiles, and sing to Your name." And again he says: "Rejoice, O Gentiles, with His people!" And again: "Praise the LORD, all you Gentiles! Laud

Him, all you peoples!" (Rom. 15:8-11). God will have this praise to its full, both now and forever. He is quoting the prophetic psalms. Gentiles are commanded to praise God singing psalms.

[3] Corporate Worship publicly acknowledges, in light of all other people, the glory of the Lord. "...in His temple everyone says, "Glory!"" (Psa. 29:9). This is much better than secret knowledge that one keeps to themselves. It is more manifest, more openly proclaimed.

Take a deplorable wretch, a wicked servant of the devil, wash his sins through the Redeemer, regenerate him through the Spirit, translate him from the dominion of darkness into the kingdom of Christ, place him in the midst of the corporate assembly for worship, have him sing psalms, new songs from this perspective, publicly with other redeemed sinners; this is very God-glorifying and Christ exalting. He is now a stone of testimony for all to see. And this greatly glorifies God. "I will declare Your name to My brethren; In the midst of the assembly I will praise You," (Psa. 22:22). This verse is also quoted by the author of Hebrews in the exaltation of Christ in corporate worship.

Testimonies are markers for others to see and hear. God is much more glorified by the collective whole than he is by the individual in secret when such testimony is accomplished with a right heart, and in the midst of the great assembly. This argues for the perfect, sublime and divine worship in the assembly of those already in the celestial city in heaven. Hold that thought for a moment.

[4] God specially attends corporate worship above all other kinds of worship. First, in his promises and exhortations. This is collectively in the church. "May the LORD our God be with us," (1 Kings 8:57). "For the LORD will not forsake His people, for His great name's sake, because it has pleased the LORD to make you His people," (1 Sam. 12:22). "I am with you always, even to the end of the age," (Matt. 28:20).

Second, in his ordinances. In their usefulness with one another. "Then all the people answered together and said, "All that the LORD has spoken we will do," (Exod. 19:8). "Oh, magnify the LORD with me, and let us exalt His name together," (Psa. 34:3). "With their voices they shall sing together; For they shall see eye to eye When the LORD brings back Zion," (Isa. 52:8).

Third, in his sacraments. In their unique station in the church. "Therefore when you come together in one place, it is not to eat the Lord's Supper. For in eating, each one takes his own supper ahead of others; and one is hungry and another is drunk," (1 Cor. 11:20-21). Here we find individuals rebuked for not collectively worshipping in the right manner. "Then He took the cup, and gave thanks, and gave it to them, saying, "Drink from it, all of you," (Matt. 26:27). Ministers dispense these mysteries publicly, and they are not regularly dispensed individually in private; they are for the whole body.

Fourth, in his ministerial offices. We find this in the exercise of the marks of the church. Why are there ministers? "...for the equipping of the saints for the work of ministry, for the edifying of the body of Christ," (Eph. 4:12). "How then shall they call on Him in whom they have not believed? And how shall they believe in Him of whom they have not heard? And how shall they hear without a preacher?" (Rom. 10:14). How would such things occur on some individual basis alone? God exercises his condescension in ministry to his church more than in any other way.

[5] Christ's atonement is specifically attached to the mystical Body ultimately as a corporate people. "So the priest shall make atonement for them, and it shall be forgiven them," (Lev. 4:20). The worship of the church in the Old Testament was a type of the work of the Messiah who would fulfill the type. Such things were not for Philistines, Jebusites, and Amorites. Sacrifices were types for God's people; his church. "So we, being many, are one body in Christ," (Rom. 12:5). "There is one body and one Spirit, just as you were called in one hope of your calling; one Lord, one faith, one baptism; one God and Father of all, who is above all, and through all, and in you all. But to each one of us grace was given according to the measure of Christ's gift," (Eph. 4:4-7). "And let the peace of God rule in your hearts, to which also you were called in one body;" (Col. 3:15). Christ died

for his church! He died for, "the church of God which He purchased with His own blood," (Acts 20:28). "For You were slain, and have redeemed us to God by Your blood Out of every tribe and tongue and people and nation," (Rev. 5:9). "For Christ has not entered the holy places made with hands, which are copies of the true, but into heaven itself, now to appear in the presence of God for us;" (Heb. 9:24). "...to Him be glory in the church by Christ Jesus to all generations, forever and ever. Amen." (Eph. 3:21).

America is a very individualistic society, where there is a great demonic attempt to individualize everything. God is looking, in opposition, for collective praise that transcends the bounds of the temporary. Individuals are certainly saved, but individuals make up the body of Christ.

[6] Corporate worship resembles the *not yet* of Christ's heavenly fulfillment and consummation. Praise in corporate worship is a snapshot, or picture of heaven. "There is a river whose streams shall make glad the city of God, The holy place of the tabernacle of the Most High. God is in the midst of her," (Psa. 46:4-5). "Then I will give them one heart, and I will put a new spirit within them, and take the stony heart out of their flesh, and give them a heart of flesh, that they may walk in My statutes and keep My judgments and do them; and they shall be My people, and I will be their God," (Ezek. 11:19-20). What will God do, "then I will give them one heart and one way, that they may fear Me forever," (Jer. 32:39).

There we will find multitudes together in worship forever. "...for the Lamb who is in the midst of the throne will shepherd them and lead them to living fountains of waters," (Rev. 7:17), to dwell with them, in their midst, "in the midst of the seven lampstands One like the Son of Man," (Rev. 1:13). In the midst of the church now, and in the midst of the church forever there the Lord Jesus receives his worship from his collective saints.

Praise, in such a wonderous understanding, is the time in which when singing psalms is new. It is new to the Christian to consider that the corporate body of Christ, in the midst of the local congregation, praises in such a manner as to give people a snapshot of eternity. Missing praise in this light to God, in a canceled service or prayer meeting and such, is like missing heaven. Psalm 96:1, alone, in a "new light" takes on a "new meaning" in the way Christians sing to the Lord. But it is *not* new; and yet, but it *is new.* For the Christian is constantly, in the mercy of the Spirit, seeing the same old bible, in *a new way.* When any psalm, hymn, or song is sung, when new spiritual glasses and new truth and new times of learning something fresh about Christ, new is new, but...the Scriptures never change. How shall this corporate blessing, then, be applied to us?

You too should desire corporate worship as the most beneficial kind of praise. If God prefers corporate worship over private, so should you. That does not mean leaving anything undone as God so requires: Bible reading, praying, godly meditation, family worship, which is like a little church. But those private exercises enable people to come to public worship, together, in a more fitting manner: they come ready to praise. That means you are more fit to come to the table, to come to hear the word, to come to pray, to come to receive blessings in the place where, on the earth now, God is manifested most and ministers to us most.

Private devotions enable people to better worship corporately. And if God loves his public worship in such a way, you should think about your private devotions as a means to an end. Your private devotions enhance public worship and public ordinances.

Christ is the author of eternal life for you. Turretin said, "Christ is in the midst of the church (as a more honorable and suitable place to be near all and diffuse his life-giving power among all; to be seen by all, as the center in which all the lines of faith and love ought to meet, that they may acquiesce in him."[2] Therefore, we say there is no salvation outside the church. Christ is dispensed there. Christ is found there. How will you find him without a preacher? How will you find him there without the truth? And if God is more interested and glorified by you in the midst of the great congregation, in the mist of his praise there, what kind of view should you have towards the church, it ministry

---

[2] Turretin, Francis, *Institutes of Elenctic Theology*, Vol. 1, (Phillipsburg, NJ: Presbyterian and Reformed Publishing Company, 1992-94) 587.

and ordinances? The Lord Jesus Christ *is in the midst* of the candlesticks; in the midst of the churches, where there are the ordinances of God. And if you want to find him, you must find him there. Psalm 68:24, "They have seen thy goings O God, even the going of my God, my King," (where is this?), "in the sanctuary." If you want to find him more clearly and experience him more deeply, then you have to know where he is, and go there.

This throws off the misguided sayings of people who say that they are put off by organized religion. In true religion, they are saying, then, they are put off by God, because that's where God is found, in the midst of his church, not in the midst of their house, or by their pool, or in their backyard.

Christ loves to be in the midst of his people. The Anointed Savior is held out there. He is in the ordinances and duties of corporate worship. Christ is in the midst of you corporately, each time you worship in the assembly. Like when the sons of God gathered together in Job in worship in the church and God was in their midst and even the devil came to accuse Job in the very midst of worship. There is much going on in the corporate assembly; but its chief end is the praise of God. God is there by the powerful working of his Holy Spirit of grace. It is an operation by an agent that he uses on you at this present time; it is from heaven, through the power of the Spirit, to you, having a presence in the midst of you, as a mystical presence in his mystical body.

The idea of the word "mystical" means supernatural, and spiritual.

The President of the United States is in his oval office. But his affect is wherever his secretaries are or his subordinate judges are. They are, for him, an effect of that power of the white house. Christ is in heaven, where he must reside until the consummation of all things. But through his sent omnipotent Spirit, he is still in the midst of his mystical body. And he supplies all spiritual benefits to them through his Spirit of Grace, and furnishes them with everything they need to become more sanctified until his return. He gives you the ability to praise in the midst of the church by his Spirit.

Christ is the center of your church life. Christ is your center as his people. He is the center of comfort, therefore called "the consolation of Israel;" he gives the "oil of joy for mourning." He is the center of love and desire, "the desire of all nations." He is the center of faith, "Our eyes are towards the Lord our God." He is the center of the mystical body, "by which they are knit together" in him. He is the center of truth, in which you receive the whole body of doctrine, being the pillar and ground of the truth as the church. He is the center of praise, where all the worship of believers end, and are completed in him. And so, it is *new*, a new song. Psalm 96 is sung to him from this view, "Worthy is the Lamb..." Such things in the church become a taste of heaven to you now. You taste them in your praise of him. It is because corporate worship and praise is a snapshot of heaven.

Want to taste heaven? Do you want to experience a bit of heaven? Sing a new song in love to God; sing as God directs; praise as he desires. You will at times taste heaven. Sometimes with the mind, sometimes with the mind and the heart, sometimes more with the emotions; sometimes more of one than the other. And you experience this in the communication of Jesus Christ in love to your soul; and so you love him back. No other praise is acceptable to God without praise drenched in divine love.

Praise is an act of love and delight. It is where you admire God, and admire all the wonderful brilliance in the truth you come to know, of that glorious being whom you love, being very deeply affected with his goodness to you. Those that are affected with such devoted praise to God will praise with happiness.

I want to give you a word of warning, that you do not lose the "newness" and sense of such godly praise to God out of fear and anxiety. You should not allow your praise ever to deteriorate into groveling and discouragement. Godly fear and rejoicing must go hand in hand. One cannot really praise with a happy countenance if they live in servile dejection to God's awesome character. Some people think that is eminently spiritual, where, wrongly viewed, it is a detriment. God is to be feared, but rightly, and if you bring Christ in your praise, then it is done with great happiness. God has shown himself in condescension to you. He has stooped down to deliver Christ to you. You bring Christ in all your worship to him, because through Christ God dwells with us. Thomas Manton said, "There are naturally in our hearts fears, estrangedness, and backwardness away from God. But now God is incarnate, and has been manifested in our flesh, we may have more familiar thoughts of him, and they are made more sweet and acceptable to us."[3]

In this, we should be thinking that in such peace and reconciliation, it makes our praise in Psalm 96, in that new song to us, *Spirit fashioned grace,* and it should be confirmed in our heart more and more. Romans 5:1-2 says, "Being justified by faith, we have peace with God, through Jesus Christ our Lord." So, sing this new song to the Lord. Sing to him all the earth.

Corporate public worship is preferred by God over private worship because praise now is a taste of heaven. Your praise now is not the end because as a Christian, you prefer heaven. You are passing by in this earthly journey on your way to the celestial city. Do you see the gates in the distance? Your *Hallelujahs* now, point to the fullness of what comes later. Imagine Christ's mystical body joined together in praise forever to him in her midst, and you standing there with everyone else? You will rejoice, glory, praise, in an everlasting future, forever, without end. Praise goes on

---

[3] Manton, Thomas, *The Complete Works of Thomas Manton,* Volume 1, (Worthington, IL: Maranatha Publications, 1979) 408.

forever. God cannot be made better than he is now, or ever has been. He is the Lord who does not change. "I the Lord change not." But he gathers around him people like you to praise him, that his glory would be made more public. More public, with more people, with new songs like Psalm 96, from the end of the earth.

Do you think that Psalm 96, to a newly regenerated Christian is a new song? The Psalms alone are like a little Bible replete and full with Christ from beginning to end. We more praise the actual name of Christ in the Psalms than any other place of any other uninspired songbook. And in heaven, his public glory is made perfect and perpetual by everyone.

The cries of hell are perpetually drowned out in heaven by the corporate praise of Christ. Those in hell are tormented by the praise of heaven; to hear such corporate praise makes hell worse for them. It is a state of praise that shall never end, and so, you should desire that; though you have a taste now, you long for the day in which such praise will be perfected later for all time.

What celestial mysteries have been revealed to the saints who have just stepped into that realm forever? It will be in heaven that God's glory will be manifested in the face of Christ most. All his people, in one accord, together, praising him for his covenant blessings. The covenant made from the foundations of the world, tasted by you now, fulfilled in heaven. It is that everlasting covenant. It is so grand, Richard Sibbes said, "that the angels themselves admire it, the devils envy it, and it is a matter of glory and praise in heaven for ever."[4] But know, it starts right here.

What would such praise sound like in heaven in that corporate congregation aided by the holy angels? What does it sound like to you now, while you wait for that day? Engage in praise now in God's corporate assembly, that you might taste what it will be like later on. Prepare such times of worship by private devotions, so that you are prepared now, that such worship today, or any Lord's Day, is another step in the direction of heaven. Because corporate worship is a picture of the eternal nature of praise to God through Christ's redemption. And so, we see that the public worship of God's people is a snapshot of the eternity of praise in heaven.

---

[4] Sibbes, Richard, *The Works of Richard Sibbes*, Volume 6, (Edinburgh: Banner of Truth Trust, 1982) 485.

Mark 5: Church Membership

"Take heed therefore unto yourselves, and to all the flock, over the which the Holy Ghost hath made you overseers, to feed the church of God, which he hath purchased with his own blood," (Acts 20:28).

This particular "unpopular topic" ought to have its own book. But in relationship to biblical commitment to the church, we need to spend a chapter on this heartily biblical doctrine.

We find in Acts 20 the final ministry of Paul to the Ephesian elders. First, he calls for the elders of the church of Ephesus (v. 17). There are elders at this church overseeing those who attend the church. In calling for those elders, he assumed that those elders were elders in a particular area having *governance and authority* over particular people. There is a church at Ephesus, a visible manifestation of the invisible church in a geographic location.

Second, he substantiates his authoritative ministry among them, and its particular nature. With prayers, tears, preaching, proclamation, serving the Lord in humility, evading the hard-hearted Jews who wanted constantly to kill him, declaring to them the whole counsel of God in a relatively short time. He preaches repentance towards God and faith in Christ.

In verses 23-25 he mentions the Holy Spirit's direction and leading in providentially sending him into the lion's den of Jerusalem, to bear witness to the truth, where these Ephesian elders will see him no more. As a consequence of this, he requires the elders, by apostolic commission, to do something very specific and important.

Third, verse 28 says, "Therefore take heed to yourselves and to all the flock, among which the Holy Spirit has made you overseers, to shepherd the church of God which He purchased with His own blood," (Acts 20:28). They are to *take heed* of themselves. This being the focused attention of being watchful as elders in the church. This means they are to take heed, be watchful, and not miss those things that will both deliver them and their flock to heaven into the arms of Christ. These Ephesian elders have received supernatural gifts completely enabling them to the whole work of the ministry in the church. If they were not qualified to work this work, nor have been given authority to do so, they would not be able to take heed of themselves or the flock.

They are to take heed *of the flock*. What flock is this? Who might they take heed over? Could there be any question in their mind who they might take heed over or be watchful over in the church at Ephesus at this point? Are they confused as to who they watch over? Could this be a point of contention? They are particularly reminded of their ordination, that the Holy Spirit has made them, ordained them, set them apart, as overseers over the flock at Ephesus. This shows that both the Holy Spirit knew who the members were at the church at Ephesus, in order to set over that flock, this ordained group of elders who were commissioned and ordained for that purpose. The Spirit knew it and the ordained elders knew it. It is *particular,* where the Greek term used denotes that they were *in and by these people,* taken from *among them and made elders over them.*

This reminding and commission to do their duty as elders, as overseers, is set in the context of sheep and those shepherding. The people who are publicly covenanted at the church at Ephesus have overseers who shepherd them. They are to shepherd these called out ones, from among the cities of Ephesus, who have come together into a discernable flock, and feed them with knowledge and understanding. There is no doubt that Paul is alluding to Jeremiah 3:15, "And I will give you shepherds according to My heart, who will feed you with knowledge and understanding." Their duty as shepherds is to do this, having the grave responsibility of overseeing this particular group of people, who were blood bought by Jesus Christ.

This blood bought group, this church, was preserved and purchased by Jesus Christ. Literally, *he made these people for himself.* He preserved them, made them living stones set on the living cornerstone and gives them the vitality of life through the Spirit. Christ remains over them as Lord of his church. He cares and guides them *by* these Ephesian elders. As the elders lead and guide, so it is the same as if Christ is leading and guiding, so long as they teach them knowledge of the word, and feed them God's teaching. So, these overseers are to remain over the flock and feed them as under shepherds to Jesus Christ the Chief Shepherd.

It is important to note, that the elders of Ephesus were to exercise authority over specific people in a specific geographical location. They did not minister personally in Rome, or Colossae. All the elders had their specific duties among particular people which they were set apart by the Holy Spirit to tend the flock of God. How could these people in the various congregations of Ephesus be watched over, or heeded, by the elders, having such authority over them, appointed by the Spirit, if the elders did not know who they were to govern, and who they should watch over? What benefit would there be by Paul exhorting the elders to exercise a dominion and authority granted in their ordination by Christ through the church over these people in Ephesus if they had no real authority over them? They would not be able, then, to tell them what to do and how to live. An Ephesian Christian might say, "I want to do this." The elders in turn may say back, "No, you need to do this as Scripture directs." How could they do this if they did not know who these people were, or have authority over them?

Is there any mention, here in these verses, of the will of the people, so to speak? Or, is this a solemn charge to the *elders* to *oversee* the flock by the Apostle to them? If they have no authority over these people in Ephesus, what would then be the point of separating them for the work of the ministry, over particular people, set apart by God's providence, and the Holy Spirit's direction? Simply, how did the elders of the Ephesian church, to which they were overseers and shepherds, able to do their ordained job? It is explicitly recorded by Luke that elders were appointed in every church (Acts 14:23) and were lawfully ordained by the laying on of the hands of other elders. Timothy was ordained in this manner over the people, "Do not neglect the gift that is in you, which was given to you by prophecy with the laying on of the hands of the eldership," (1 Tim. 4:14). Elders ordain elders and set them apart. Such ministers are separated by the Holy Spirit and set over the people to lead and teach them. "As they ministered to the Lord and fasted, the Holy Spirit said, "Now separate to Me Barnabas and Saul for the work to which I have called them,"" (Acts 13:2). Each individual church in Ephesus, or any visible church mentioned in Scripture, were ministered to by Jesus Christ, by the power of the Holy Spirit, through local elders who have rule, governance, spiritual authority, over the people. Christ had set apart these men manifesting to each of them, and the church, the visibility of their gifts, and the inward desire for the office itself as Jeremiah 3, Job 33, 1 Timothy 3 and Titus 1 directs. Christ appointed them to take care of these churches. Consider Christ's exhortation to the elders of Ephesus in Rev. 2:3, "and you have persevered and have patience, and have labored for My name's sake and have not become weary," (Rev. 2:3). His angels, his ministers, are complimented due to their duty over the church, his candlesticks of Revelation, and wherever each candlestick was related, in this case Ephesus; Christ had visible, geographic churches, which specific elders had care of and governed by authority.

These churches, then, are made up of specific people, brought out of the world, into the governed institution of Christ, called *the church*. Even Christ recognizes these elders who rule over these specific groups of people. This is why Paul called the ordained elders, the shepherds, to exhort them to watch over their own souls, and the souls that they have charge over. Such a power over Christ's flock, over his church, is a spiritual power, ratified by the blood of the everlasting covenant of the Anointed Savior. It is a manifestation of the solemn vow of covenanting with God, his government, his people, his church and those he has placed over them for their good.

Questions then arise. What kind of people are these that these Ephesian elders have charge over? And, how do elders have charge over specific people?

The divine origin and institution of the Christian ministry by Jesus Christ through ordained elders presupposes covenanted church members. Elders are appointed by the Father (1 Cor. 12:28), given to the church by the Son (Eph. 4:11-12), and ordained as ministers and empowered for the church by the direction of the Holy Spirit (Acts 20:28). Jesus is not remiss in ordering his blood bought church; God is a God of order. He is not remiss in those leading it, and those governed under that leadership. These ordained men are called:

Ambassadors for Christ, (2 Cor. 5:20)

Angels of the Church, (Rev. 1:20; 2:1)

Defenders of the Faith, (Phil. 1:7)

Elders, (1 Tim. 5:17; 1 Pet. 5:1)

Laborers, (Matt. 9:38, with Philem. 1)

Lights, (John 5:35)

Messengers, (2 Cor. 8:23)

Messengers of the Lord, (Mal. 2:7)

Ministers of God, (Isa. 61:6; 2 Cor. 6:4)

Ministers of the Lord, (Joel 2:17)

Ministers of Christ, (Rom. 15:16; 1 Cor. 4:1)

Ministers of the Word, (Luke 1:2)

Ministers of Righteousness, (2 Cor. 11:15)

Overseers of God's people, (Acts 20:28)

Pastors, (Jer. 3:15; John 21:16–18; Eph. 4:11)

Preachers, (Rom. 10:14; 1 Tim. 2:7)

Preachers of Righteousness, (2 Pet. 2:5)

Stewards of God, (Titus 1:7)

...and a variety of other important designations in both the Old Testament and New Testament. They have a specific calling, certain qualifications, are charged by God to accomplish their ministry (answerable to Christ), have certain duties to fulfill, and are set over a specific geographical church made up of covenanted disciples. They are to be ordained to their office, tested, prayed for to fulfill their God-given duties, and are to be zealous for God's word and the Gospel of Jesus Christ. In considering such an office in the church, the Scriptures attached to its duty the exhortation to take heed of both themselves and to those they have been entrusted. *Take heed, to watch over.* Those entrusted to them, are a specific kind of people in a specific geographic location. This is what further needs to be explored.

The visible church of Jesus Christ is comprised of covenanted members. They are, in fact, converted members. "And the Lord added to the church daily those who were being saved," (Acts 2:47). "Now when the Gentiles heard this, they were glad and glorified the word of the Lord. And as many as had been appointed to eternal life believed," (Acts 13:48). What are they added to, but the visible body of the church in a geographic area.

These converted people have a Christian profession of faith. "Then He said to Thomas, "Reach your finger here, and look at My hands; and reach your hand here, and put it into My side. Do not be unbelieving, but believing." And Thomas answered and said to Him, "My Lord and my God!"" (John 20:27-28). "Therefore God also has highly exalted Him and given Him the name which is above every name, that at the name of Jesus every knee should bow, of those in heaven, and of those on earth, and of those under the earth, and that every tongue should confess that Jesus Christ is

Lord, to the glory of God the Father." (Phil. 2:9-11). And to whom do they profess? Their profession is implied under the governing of the church; Thomas in particular to Jesus Christ the chief Shepherd, and others to the elders of a church before their fellow Christians.

Public profession has always been a normal part of congregational worship. "To declare the name of the LORD in Zion, And His praise in Jerusalem," (Psa. 102:21). Why? As a profession of belief in certain understood non-negotiable biblical doctrines one of which is that Jesus Christ is the only Savior. Such as: God is triune, that they are sinful, that they are submissive to Christ's rule and reign, that Christ alone saves and that God alone justifies the ungodly.

These people are covenanted and confessing together. What does it mean to covenant with one another in a visible church? These are very evil days, and perilous times. There are many sins that attribute themselves to making the times very evil and very perilous. Sins of perilous and evil times are the following: being, "filled with all unrighteousness, sexual immorality, wickedness, covetousness, maliciousness, full of envy, murder, strife, deceit, evil-mindedness, whisperers, backbiters, haters of God, violent, proud, boasters, inventors of evil things, disobedient to parents, undiscerning, untrustworthy, unloving, truce-breakers, unmerciful..." (Rom. 1:29-32). In 2 Timothy 3:3 Paul uses a term "truce-breakers" as well. "Without natural affection, trucebreakers, false accusers, incontinent, fierce, despisers of those that are good," (2 Tim. 3:3). Other translations outside of the Greek and the KJV use an aberrant word such as *unforgiving*, which is an extremely poor way to convey the idea. The Greek word is ἄσπονδοι, which is literary rendered "one who will not be persuaded to enter into a covenant." Paul marks this sin among 19 sins in this section of 2 Timothy as sins of perilous times, and 23 sins of Romans 1 of the evil day where God gives people over to a reprobate mind. Those who *refuse to enter into a covenant together with a church*, to join it, specifically under the context of the worker who works among the people of God in 2 Timothy, and in perilous times where sin abounds, *is a covenant breaker* – a truce-breaker. Paul names all sorts of sins, but this sin of covenant breaking and covenant keeping is one in which directly affects the membership of Christ's church.

In Romans 1:31 Paul lists this same covenant breaking sin in line with giving people over to a reprobate mind; part of God's judgment. "Without understanding, covenant breakers, without natural affection, *etc.*" (Rom. 1:31). It is a very serious sin. It is a sin of those who willfully reject God's authority, and his imposed authority in the church. It is a sin of pride. It is the description of a sin of people who do not want to be part of the membership role of a church.

The tenth sin listed in this long line of sins in 2 Timothy that make the times perilous, is rendered as those who *refuse to enter into church covenant.* This could also take on, those breaking covenant. People say, "I don't like this church anymore, I'm just going to go to another one somewhere else." To be one who is a truce-breaker or covenant-refuser is a perilous sin that adds to the evil of the day. This applies both to covenant-breakers, and those who hate the peace of the church which is regulated by the elders of the church in spiritual discipline.

Godly *covenanting* in the context of the church means committing one's self verbally and publicly to God's church and people – a professing Christian – who upholds the church in their profession. ""Therefore, keep the words of this covenant, and do them, that you may prosper in all that you do. "All of you stand today before the LORD your God: your leaders and your tribes and your elders and your officers, all the men of Israel, "your little ones and your wives-- also the stranger who is in your camp, from the one who cuts your wood to the one who draws your water-- "that you may enter into covenant with the LORD your God, and into His oath, which the LORD your God makes with you today, "that He may establish you today as a people for Himself, and that He may be God to you," (Deut. 29:9-13). This is a command and is all inclusive.

It should be a joyous covenanting together as found in 2 Chronicles 15:14-15, "Then they took an oath before the LORD with a loud voice, with shouting and trumpets and rams' horns. And all Judah rejoiced at the oath, for they had sworn with all their heart and sought

Him with all their soul; and He was found by them, and the LORD gave them rest all around."

Such a covenanting work should be serious towards reformation. This is how it was in the days of Josiah. "Now the king sent them to gather all the elders of Judah and Jerusalem to him. The king went up to the house of the LORD with all the men of Judah, and with him all the inhabitants of Jerusalem-- the priests and the prophets and all the people, both small and great. And he read in their hearing all the words of the Book of the Covenant which had been found in the house of the LORD. Then the king stood by a pillar and made a covenant before the LORD, to follow the LORD and to keep His commandments and His testimonies and His statutes, with all his heart and all his soul, to perform the words of this covenant that were written in this book. And all the people took a stand for the covenant," (2 Kings 23:1-3). The Christian should say, "Put me down on that roll; I take a stand in it."

It is perilous times where a person in their home professes to be a Christian yet will not join with others publicly in that profession as a church member. Even seen prophetically in Jeremiah 4:2, "And you shall swear, 'The LORD lives,' In truth, in judgment, and in righteousness; The nations shall bless themselves in Him, And in Him they shall glory.'" Even in prophecy, in Gospel times, vowing is to take place as commanded by God, "you shall swear." They say, "Well, I don't want to do that." Well, then, you are not fulfilling God's requirement of a professing Christian. Such a rebel contributes to the perilous sins of the day.

Who, then, shall they vow to? They are members under the authority of the Christ, through his under-shepherds. "Let the elders who rule well be counted worthy of double honor, especially those who labor in the word and doctrine," (1 Tim. 5:17). They submit to the elders of the church who govern them; they are a governed people. "And we urge you, brethren, to recognize those who labor among you, and are over you in the Lord and admonish you, and to esteem them very highly in love for their work's sake," (1 Thess. 5:12-13). These Christians should have a high esteem for their work. "Remember those who rule over you, who have spoken the word of God to you, whose faith follow, considering the outcome of their conduct," (Heb. 13:7). These elders rule over people. "Obey those who rule over you, and be submissive, for they watch out for your souls, as those who must give account. Let them do so with joy and not with grief, for that would be unprofitable for you," (Heb. 13:17). People don't like that word *obey*. Obey them. The church is not to be run with some kind of gym-membership mentality. One comes in, tries things out for some thirty days, or 30 years, and then decides they don't want to work out anymore so they leave. Covenanted members do not get to simply walk out of a church. This is why many professing Christians do not want to join a church – it is because they are mere professors. They do not want to be subject to godly authority who can tell them what they can and cannot do before the Lord.

Christians are governed in a church, have oversight in that church, have privileges in that church, and are to be submissive in that church to the elders as a covenanted member who has vowed to do so publicly. They are to take a stand in that covenant before the eyes and ears of others. Otherwise, without this, there is no need for governing of any kind in the church. If governing souls, taking heed to them, is something the Lord requires of his elders, then the opposite is biblically unsound, and it is sinful – *a perilous sin,* "...knowing the righteous judgment of God, that those who practice such things are deserving of death," (Rom. 1:32). "...having a form of godliness but denying its power. And from such people turn away!" (2 Tim. 3:5).

Public swearing or oath taking (covenanting) is commanded, "You shall fear the LORD your God and serve Him, and shall take oaths in His name," (Deut. 6:13). People are to vow by way of a solemn oath to uphold the truth and practice of their church.

I offer to you even a side note: such people are recorded members of a church on the church roll. The idea of the "book" of the testimony of the people of God runs throughout all of Scripture in various ways, even amidst a cursory reading of it. It's the membership role, if you will. To the church in Sardis the Lord Jesus writes that He will not "blot out his name from the Book of Life" who is faithful and obedient to the Lord. Revelation 13:8;

17:8; 20:12,15; also refer to the Book of Life in general – that God has a book. God has books, with names, so to speak, written down, and recorded.

In the Old Testament there were many membership rolls with the names of all the covenant families and the covenant heads of households. Genesis 5:1ff speaks of the "book of the generations." In Exodus 24:7 we read of the "Book of the Covenant" which contained the laws by which God's covenant people were to live; the book they were to follow. God commanded Moses to take a census of the church and to make a record of them (Exodus 30:11). Psalm 87:6 speaks of God making a, "register of the peoples." Ezekiel 13:9 says, "My hand will be against the prophets who envision futility and who divine lies; they shall not be in the assembly of My people, nor be written in the record of the house of Israel, nor shall they enter into the land of Israel. Then you shall know that I am the Lord GOD," (Ezek. 13:9). False prophets are not part of the church's role. God had his people keep records of covenant keepers and covenant breakers, so that they would know who they were.

Even in the New Testament Church there was the problem of the distribution of food in Acts 6:1, they had to keep record of those eligible widows who needed help. They knew who they were because they were on the roll. In 1 Timothy 5:9–16 Paul speaks plainly about a list of Christian widows who received financial assistance from the Church. These qualifications were to be listed and recorded. "Let not a widow be taken into the number," (1 Tim. 5:9). People just don't think about some of these things as it relates to the church's orderly organization.

These people are covenanted members under discipline, either corrective of preventative. "This punishment which was inflicted by the majority is sufficient for such a man, so that, on the contrary, you ought rather to forgive and comfort him, lest perhaps such a one be swallowed up with too much sorrow," (2 Cor. 2:6-7). They had disciplined the sexually immoral man, from 1 Cor. 5, "that he was rebuked of many." Discipline is either preventative or corrective. Discipline is not begrudging, it is correcting sometimes in hard love. It is mostly preventative. Sermons are preventative discipline to lead the church into upholding covenanted membership, and not to break it; preventative against sinning in this manner. For a church not to hold this privilege in high regard, given to them, by the crucified and resurrected Christ, commanded that they do such to glorify Him, is to sin wickedly and rebel against God.

Covenanting in the church, joining the church, in a local area, is housed upon and in obedience to the Word of God, and it carries with it the discipline of the church ordained elders who oversee it. Sometimes it is at great lengths, as in Matthew 18, and sometimes it is biblically quick as in 1 Corinthians 5 or Titus 3:10; discipline in many cases is to be made known to the whole body. The Body? Who should know? Who is the body? The man who had been cast out in 1 Cor. 5, is reinstated. Reinstated, where? "Wherefore, I pray you...confirm your love towards him." John 13:35, "By this shall all men know, that ye are my disciples, if ye have love one to another." Who is the *one another?* By Paul's direction, because of the man's repentance, of which we do not have a specific account, he exhorts the Corinthians to take the man back (back where?), and show him an exceeding abundance of love (from whom?). Those who had cast him out (cast him out of where), and handed him over to Satan and the world must now receive him back with the love of Christ. It had reached Paul that he repented! Where did he get such information? In regard to *what* place?

Church discipline is a privilege of membership in the church. Why a privilege? It is for a Christian's good because it is instituted by Christ himself. Jesus died for the church, and very much cares that it is governed and watched over in a manner of godliness. Christ never says that his church is to be filled with corruption. It is to be discernably purged of it; one cannot be excommunicated from *nothing* unless he is a member of that *something.*

Discipline in the church is for edification: whether preventative or corrective. It keeps a Christian from straying from Christ and sinning against his body and blood. Anything which does this is a blessing because being kept from sin is a grace.

Covenanted members in a local church can be excommunicated from the church, but non-covenanted members cannot. From what? *From the church*. From their covenanting in it. What good would it have done, in any way to cast the man out of the church in 1 Cor. 5 if he could simply waltz down the street to another church with no repercussions?

These people are privileged members who are collectively interested in God's agenda in a specific geographical location; this rests heartily on Acts 2.

There are privileges to membership in the church that one does not get without it. They are allowed to use their gifts to love one another in service in a particular place; they know who they minister to. They meet together for public worship and teaching lead by church governors in a particular place (Acts 20:7; 1 Cor. 14:23, 26, 34, 35). The privilege of the preaching of the word by those ordained and qualified in a particular place (Rom. 1:15; 1 Cor. 15:11-14; 2 Tim. 4:2). They pray for one another, (Acts 1:14; 12:5; Rom. 12:12; 15:30; Col. 4:2-3). They fellowship together, (Acts 2:42; 2 Pet. 2:13; 1 John 1:3; Jude 12). They tithe to support the church. They support their minister, their church, and the poor around them, (Acts 2:44-45; 6:1-6; Rom. 15:26; 1 Cor. 9:4-14; 2 Cor. 9:1-15; Gal. 2:10; James 2:15-16). They support orphans and widows (1 Tim. 5:3, 16; James 1:27). They partake of the ordinances of God, like baptism, which are the ordinances of Christ. (The life of the Christian is a godly sermon, a practical outworking of improving their baptism or of exemplifying it. But who do they do this to?) And what of the Lord's Supper (1 Cor. 11:18-34)?

Paul admonishes the church to know who is partaking, whether such partaking is valid or not by examination. How does anyone know if examination has personally occurred, unless there is some governing of those examining themselves?

These people are members of the church who are spiritually watched over. Consider, "And when Saul had come to Jerusalem, he tried to join the disciples; but they were all afraid of him, and did not believe that he was a disciple," (Acts 9:26). *Join*, means, literally *to glue himself to them*; to fasten and cleave. That is why the phrase "join a church" is on point. Christians are to be glued to it. "Obey those who rule over you, and be submissive, for they watch out for your souls, as those who must give account. Let them do so with joy and not with grief, for that would be unprofitable for you," (Heb. 13:17). *Obey* means to be persuaded and to comply, and the phrase "be submissive" is better translated as "do not resist them." The governors of the church are not instructed by God to do this for everyone in the world, but only for the *members* of the church in a given location.

You must realize the benefits of church covenanting and membership. Benefits are only attached to privileges. Christ commands you, as one under authority, to solemnly vow publicly of your intention to serve him in your church. There are private vows you can make, but those are things like personal fasts, promises between you and the Lord, and such, are not this public vow. You cannot be indifferent to Christ's teaching concerning the body, and his government of it. You would, then, be indifferent to a brother or sister who may need your counsel. Or, indifferent to the use of your gifts. Or, indifferent to the elders who teach you the word. If ministers labor, well, then, you labor. It is dangerous to indulge in indifference in solemn and important matters like this; and to reject it is to cultivate the sin of pride.

The sacraments are benefits of the church and they are used in a manner for spiritual well-being and governing over you. Can you administer baptism and the Lords Supper yourself? Baptism, "The outward element to be used in this sacrament is water, wherewith the party is to be baptized in the name of the Father, and of the Son, and of the Holy Ghost, by a minister of the gospel lawfully called thereunto."[1] The Lord's Supper, "The Lord Jesus hath, in this ordinance, appointed his ministers to declare his word of institution to the people, to pray, and bless the elements of bread and wine, and thereby to set them apart from a common to an holy use; and to take and break the bread, to take the cup, and (they communicating also themselves) to give both to the communicants; but to none who are not then present in the congregation."[2] This is because the

---

[1] *1647 Westminster Confession of Faith* 28:2, *cf.* Matt. 3:11; 28:19-20; John 1:33.

[2] *1647 Westminster Confession of Faith* 29:3, *cf.* Matt. 26:26-28 and Mark 14:22-24 and Luke 22:19-20 with 1 Cor. 11:23-27; Acts 20:7; 1 Cor 11:20.

ordinances surround the assumption that you are a believer and you are converted; you have received Christ and have been examined in such things; John 1:12, "as many as have received him." It assumes, in the cases of adults, "Repent, and be baptized every one of you in the name of Jesus Christ," (Acts 2:38). It assumes in that way a public confession of faith, "That if thou shalt confess with thy mouth the Lord Jesus, and shalt believe in thine heart that God hath raised him from the dead, thou shalt be saved. For with the heart man believeth unto righteousness; and with the mouth confession is made unto salvation," (Rom. 10:9). This is not, *do this* and *be converted.* This confession is *after conversion*, in the light of the testimony of your life in the church. It shows forth a godly walk and godly knowledge in obedience. "This is love, that we walk according to His commandments. This is the commandment, that as you have heard from the beginning, you should walk in it," (2 John 1:6 and *cf.* Psalm 119:66).

What about examination? (1 Cor. 11). How would the elders of your church know this about you if you can come and go as you pleased? Jeremiah Burroughs takes a great amount of time in his work *Gospel Worship*[3] explaining why coming together and partaking of the supper with holy members is so vital to the success of the supper. They should be coming

---

[3] His work has been updated and gently modernized by Puritan Publications.

together as a covenanted group of believers who have been examined according to the measure of their faith.

And what, then shall be said of church membership? In Acts 9:26 Paul didn't come and go as he pleased. They didn't trust him in the beginning when he wanted to join the disciples and fasten to them like glue. "No, Saul, you must first be examined and tested as a Christian; then we will let you into the church and then you will be under the authority of the elders." He came and went with them *after* they examined him and allowed him into the fold. *Then* he was counted among them; he was governed by them. "And when Saul had come to Jerusalem, he tried to join the disciples; but they were all afraid of him, and did not believe that he was a disciple. *[No privileges]* But Barnabas took him and brought him to the apostles. And he declared to them how he had seen the Lord on the road, and that He had spoken to him, and how he had preached boldly at Damascus in the name of Jesus. So he was with them at Jerusalem, coming in and going out, (Acts 9:26-28). After your vow, after your joining to the church, you get to come and go in that context, in that geographic area with those people.

You must fulfill your vows. There is first sin in not vowing as a truce-breaker. Remember, those who do not want to join a church are called truce-breakers, and those that establish churches with no membership at all are called false teachers. That in and of itself is a sin of the perilous nature of the times. How applicable is this in our day? "I don't want to be told what to do. I don't want that oversight. I don't want that accountability." When we have sworn obedience to God, we must perform and observe what we have sworn to God; and lost people hate doing that. "Vow, and pay to the Lord," (Psalm 76:11). You must pay your vows; which in turn, in and of itself, rids the church of those false professors who really are not Christians. God commands you to make public vows, and fulfill them. "If a man vow a vow unto the Lord, or swear an oath to bind his soul with a bond, he shall not break his word," (Num. 30:2). Be very careful to perform what you swear to God when you join his church. And this should not put you off vowing, but simply to be more bound to do what you say. To know what you vow to – the visible representation of his mystical body in the world in a specific place.

God has sworn, has promised to you in the covenant of grace, to uphold his end of the covenant in Christ, and he is the great promise keeper. He keeps all his promises. He expects you to keep your promises as well. When we are bound by the oath of joining the church, we must fulfill that which we bind ourselves to.

There are many required duties you cannot fulfill unless you are a member of the church. Without membership, church life would be opposite to the God of order. "Let all things be done decently and in order," (1 Cor. 14:40). God is orderly in the church. Churches have a membership role to keep things orderly; to know who comes in and who goes out. Accountability would be beyond the bounds of possibility. Who would be accountable to whom? The sin of truce-breaking, individuality, would determine this instead of the elders over the body of Christ who are given the entreaty to look out for those in the flock, and bear one another's burdens. And members look out for one another as well, "You are the body of Christ and each one of you is a part of it."

Elders have rule over people. People have an obligation to submit in godly persuasion of the truth. Spiritual gifts could never be used in the local body if there were no joining it. Who is the local body? In Acts 6:1-6, they had to know who was part of the body and who was not to feasibly discern those deacons who were "full of the Holy Spirit and of wisdom." "...choose out from among you." Among whom? Who would pastors oversee? The elders of Ephesus were given oversight of specific people, not all people, or all Christians. The transient element alone of people coming and going as they pleased would disrupt any possibility of the submission of a Christian to their authority. It would render the church chaotic. That is not only a violation of the character of God, but also what he has so set down, and even so set against what the Holy Spirit has set down in 2 Timothy as the *perilous* sins of the times. How could church officers watch over the souls of the congregation if they did not know whom they were watching over? It is a preposterous, sinful, and wicked position partaking of the evils of the day to start a new church without the privilege of church membership. Much less to say, "I will not join a church. I will not submit. I will not recognize Christ's authority over me in his under shepherds. I will not be part of his body. I will not exercise my gifts among the members."

There would be the impossibility of church discipline or counseling. One cannot have exclusion in discipline from nothing. The excommunicated person has to be excluded from the identifiable body of believers. This would be wholly useless if the sin of individuality was given reign. People often say, "But I gladly submit myself under their authority."

Where does the Bible say that you are the one allowed to submit yourself at your own convenience without their consent or oversight? Titus was exhorted by Paul in Titus 3:10-11 that the church is required to "reject the heretic" after being admonished twice. The word "reject" means to "not allow the professor to be among you." In this way, excommunication in an individualistic church scheme becomes meaningless. Also, it is a conditional act to be restored which is immediately relevant to be accepted again by the body of existing covenanted members. 2 Thess. 3:6 says, "Now we command you, brethren, in the name of our Lord Jesus Christ, that ye withdraw yourselves from every brother that walketh disorderly, and not after the tradition which he received of us." This Scripture, and others like it, would be meaningless. Who are they? Who are these brothers? How do you know? Paul and

James would not have had the ability to exhort the body concerning orphans or widows if there were not some visible discerning list and discernable members of the body. Non-members do not have the privilege of discerning the Lord's body since they are not part of the body of the local church; they would not know who they are. There are a variety of problems that arise concerning the Lord's Supper when the sin of individualism dictates how 1 Cor. 11 is to be interpreted. Who is the body at that point? How can we discern the Lord's Body? What is the act of discerning? Can we discern a disjointed body which is really not a body but a transient gathering of vagabonds?

Monetary support of the church would be a nightmare; who is required to give, what should they give, when and to what church? No one would ever be able to state, with any degree of emphasis, that a person did not have the right to disperse his or her tithe among 8 churches instead of one church. If this were the case, the church would never be supported, and the elders would not be paid (though they are worthy of their wages).

Ordination of elders and deacons, as well as formal missionary work would be a nightmare. Who sends who? Who are the pastors sent out accountable to? Why are they accountable to one body and not another except for monetary support?

Christianity would become chaotic, showing, there is no such thing as a Lone Ranger Christian. If there is no covenanted membership, then the only other choice is to have autonomous Christians with no deemed authority except what they personally deem acceptable or not; that is American individualism at work. That is the sin of pride. That is the same sin that cast humanity into apostasy in the garden. All biblical covenanting falls apart with that sinful truce-breaking mindset. The very idea of a local church assumes membership in it. The outworking of those who openly profess their faith to one another, not just those who claim to be Christians and attend, are part of a local church. This profession of faith culminates in their desire to be lead and guided by their brothers and sisters in a covenant, and a submission under the officers of the church.

There is a necessary distinction that must be made, as much as is humanly possible, being led by the Word of God, between infidels and the church. Without some kind of membership process, the local church would cease and its mandate to be visibly expressive in the world as a definable community of believers and their children in any given geographic locale would be impossible. Shouldn't the local church be more organized than a sports team? And yet, many do not think so. They would rather act like Christian infidels.

On a practical note, you should never, unless there are some extenuating circumstance (such as no biblical church to attend), for any extended amount of time, not be a covenanted member of a local body of believers. Generally speaking, as to the evil of times, and the world we live in, to remain uncovenanted is to be in rebellion against Christ; it makes your church life more perilous. Josiah would have railed against anyone standing in the midst of the public vow that said, "I don't want to be part of this." He might have even put them to death along with the false prophets and priests. The Apostles would rebuke such a one. Christ calls them truce-breakers; generally speaking as it pertains to people in the world today. God requires that his people covenant together in local assemblies of like-minded doctrinal unity for the sake of edification and the propagation of the Gospel.

The elders in such places take heed of themselves and you. You must reject all the sins of the times, which includes sin #10, in the list of 2 Timothy 3:3. The logic of like-mindedness alone, and the reality of the covenant signs alone, demand unity, not separatism, or schism. The examples of the New Testament (especially Acts 15 and 21) demonstrate a regulation of the church corporately, as one full body of Christ extended into the world. All this work is based on like-mindedness and the authority of the Apostles and elders, sending out missionaries (preachers) around the world to plant churches that are like-minded, covenanted and of the same doctrine of the Apostles. Ephesus ultimately had many churches but one governance from the church of Jerusalem who sent Paul to ordain elders in every church. They took heed over those people, whom Jesus bought with his blood. Christ says the church is worth such holy oversight, for and that oversight is for the visible church comprised of *covenanted members.*

Appendix

The reader must be aware that the Bible does not give us the exact formal outline of how the church should conduct new membership classes or how to structure initiating members, *per se*. However, it does give us hints and guidelines, and leads us in certain a direction. It furnishes us with some very clear strategies, rules and commands (such as with choosing elders and deacons – see Acts 6, 1 Timothy 3 and Titus 1).

Prudence dictates that the officers of the church, session, or General Assembly of elders should create a workable and formal membership criteria for their church. If they do not, then they will be teaching, by their *non-action*, that the sin of individualism is something Christians should accept and cultivate, which is wholly against the biblical record.

Other Helpful Books
by Puritan Publications

5 Marks of a Biblical Church by C. Matthew McMahon

5 Marks of a Biblical Disciple by C. Matthew McMahon

The Reformed Apprentice Volume 4: A Workbook on Private Devotions by C. Matthew McMahon

Rules for Our Walking with God by Jeremiah Burroughs (1599-1646)

The Christian's Duty to Walk Wisely by Matthew Mead (1630-1699)

Walking Worthy of the Gospel by Nathaniel Vincent (1639-1697)

Directions for Daily Holy Living by Daniel Burgess (1645-1713)

The Zealous Christian by Simeon Ashe (d. 1662)

The Church's Need of Jesus Christ by Thomas Valentine (1586-1665)